Leaders of the Colonial Era

Miles Standish

Leaders of the Colonial Era

Leaders of the Colonial Era

Miles Standish

Daniel K. Davis

CHELSEA HOUSE
PUBLISHERS
An imprint of Infobase Publishing

MILES STANDISH
Copyright © 2011 by Infobase Publishing

Chelsea House
An imprint of Infobase Publishing
132 West 31st Street
New York, NY 10001

Library of Congress Cataloging-in-Publication Data
Davis, Daniel K.
 Miles Standish / Daniel K. Davis.
   p. cm. — (Leaders of the colonial era)
 Includes bibliographical references and index.
 ISBN 978-1-60413-739-2 (hardcover)
 1. Standish, Myles, 1584?–1656—Juvenile literature. 2. Pilgrims (New Plymouth
Colony)—Biography—Juvenile literature. 3. Soldiers—Massachusetts—
Biography—Juvenile literature. 4. Massachusetts—History—New Plymouth, 1620–
1691—Biography—Juvenile literature. I. Title. II. Series.
 F68.S87D38 2010
 974.4'02092—dc22
 [B]   2010010333

You can find Chelsea House on the World Wide Web at
http://www.chelseahouse.com

Text design by Kerry Casey
Cover design by Keith Trego
Composition by EJB Publishing Services
Cover printed by Bang Printing, Brainerd, Minn.
Book printed and bound by Bang Printing, Brainerd, Minn.
Date printed: October 2010
Printed in the United States of America

10 9 8 7 6 5 4 3 2 1

This book is printed on acid-free paper.

All links and Web addresses were checked and verified to be correct at the time of
publication. Because of the dynamic nature of the Web, some addresses and links
may have changed since publication and may no longer be valid.

Contents

1

Stranger in a Strange Land

After more than two months at sea, the *Mayflower* finally entered Cape Cod Bay, in what is today Massachusetts, on November 11, 1620. The ship's passengers were mainly Pilgrims, members of an outlawed Separatist church in England who hoped to start a new colony in America where they could practice their religion without fear of punishment.

They were thankful to reach land, but they knew their greatest trials still lay ahead of them. On November 15, 16 men from the ship set out on foot to explore an area of the cape from what today is known as Providence Harbor to Cold Harbor.

They were entering unknown territory—though they knew what sorts of dangers *could* be waiting for them on land. They weren't the first Europeans to try to settle in the New World, and those that came before them had had their share of run-ins with unwelcoming natives.

The man in charge of this risky first exploration might have seemed an unlikely leader: stocky but only about five feet (152.4 centimeters) tall, with reddish hair and a reddish complexion. He could not have seemed a very imposing figure. Yet lead he did, guiding the other New World travelers on a quest to find a suitable place to build a settlement in a strange and dangerous land.

The man was Captain Miles Standish. Besides his small size, other things set him apart from most of the other settlers. He was not a true Pilgrim. Rather, he had come to Holland—where the Pilgrims lived before leaving for the New World—not as a religious refugee but as a soldier (it's still a question as to whether he ever did join the Pilgrims' church). His clothes helped identify him as a military man. According to Kate Caffrey in her book *The Mayflower*, "Captain Standish wore a rust-brown doublet [a snug-fitting buttoned jacket] with shoulder caps, braid stripes down the sleeves, and buttoned tie fastenings, with white cuffs—Cromwell's russet-coated captain."

And then there was his personality. Miles (or "Myles," as it's sometimes spelled) Standish was known for having a very sharp temper. In his 1848 book *A General History of New England*, William Hubbard writes, "A little chimney is soon fired; so was the Plymouth Captain, a man of very little stature, yet of a very hot and angry temper." He was a man who took insults very seriously. He could be strict, ruthless, and prone to fits of violence. "The fire of his passion soon kindled and blown up into a flame by hot words," Hubbard writes, "might easily have consumed all, had it not been seasonably quenched."

Yet despite Standish's fiery personality, he was generally highly regarded among the Pilgrims, who counted on him to keep them safe from attacks by Native American tribes known to be hostile to settlers and to help maintain good relations with those known to be friendly. Though he may not have been, strictly speaking, one of the Pilgrims,

AMERICA BEFORE THE PILGRIMS

Before the Pilgrims made their way to the New World, there had been other attempts by the English to found settlements in America. It didn't take a group of colonists long to figure out that Newfoundland was not an ideal place to build their new home; they abandoned their settlement soon after founding it there in 1583. Sir Walter Raleigh made a failed attempt on Roanoke Island, off the coast of what would become North Carolina, in 1587. The supposed first birth of a white child in America, a girl named Virginia Dare, occurred here. When the settlement's leader returned from a resupply trip to England, all 117 people he had left behind were gone. The only clue to their disappearance was the word "CROATOAN" (the name of a nearby island) scratched into a fort wall. The fate of the colonists remains a mystery to this day.

Slightly more successful was the settlement of Jamestown, Virginia in 1607. The colonists there had to contend with malaria, raids by native tribes in which many settlers were killed, fighting amongst themselves, and low food supplies. Of the original 108 settlers, 70 died in the first year, and another 440 out of 500 colonists died the following winter, mainly due to starvation. And yet, this was the most successful English settlement in the New World when the Pilgrims crossed the Atlantic in 1620.

he remained completely devoted to them. His job was defending the settlement, and he worked at it tirelessly.

It is thus not surprising that the same author who called Standish a "chimney . . . soon fired" would also write of him that he was "of as good courage as conduct" and "always managed his trust with great integrity and faithfulness." Standish was a man who during his lifetime would be called "rascal," "silly boy," and "Captain Shrimp," but

Colonial leader Miles Standish was responsible for the safety and the well-being of the settlers on the *Mayflower*, later to become the community members of the Plymouth settlement. His life and persona have been immortalized in poems and popular culture, yet little is known about the man himself.

he would also win the praise and affection of his comrades for playing nurse while many of them were terribly sick.

John Robinson, the Pilgrims' minister who remained in England, perhaps best summed up the contradictions of Miles Standish. In a letter to the Pilgrims' leader William Bradford, Robinson said of Standish, "[I] am persuaded the Lord in great mercy and for much good hath sent you him, if you use him aright. He is a man humble and meek amongst you, and toward all in ordinary course. But . . . there is cause to fear that by occasion, especially of provocation, there may be wanting that tenderness of the life of man." In other words, Standish is a great man to have on your side, but look out for that temper of his.

Unfortunately we have no account of Miles Standish in his own words. We have no letters to friends or family back in England or Holland. He kept no journal, and he wrote no memoir. Thus we have to trust those who wrote about him, some of whom knew him personally, but most of whom didn't. The problem with this is, sometimes those accounts can be quite different, most notably in the case of Standish's arrest of Thomas Morton, which will be discussed later.

To add to the uncertainty, much of what people think they know about Standish is colored by the famous 1858 poem by Henry Wadsworth Longfellow, *The Courtship of Miles Standish*. Longfellow stated that the poem tells a true story, but there is little historical evidence to back up much of it. Likewise, Longfellow admits to taking some liberties with the facts. This has not, however, stopped later generations of writers from taking some events in the poem as fact, most notably the one in which Standish sends John Alden to court Priscilla Mullins for him, only to have Priscilla respond, "Why don't you speak for yourself, John?"

The result of Longfellow's poem has been a romanticized version of Standish that doesn't reflect his complexities and contradictions.

He could be a man of great compassion and devotion, but also a man of petty grudges and furious rage—at least once, to deadly ends. He is a mysterious figure whose past was not recorded until he joined the Pilgrims on the voyage of the *Mayflower*, and yet it's not even clear why he chose to join them on their perilous and uncertain journey. What is clear is that without Miles Standish in their ranks, the Pilgrims almost certainly would not have survived even their first winter in Plymouth Plantation.

2

Mysterious Origins

When examining the life of a historical figure, it often helps to explore the years before he or she became famous. Unfortunately, in the case of Miles Standish, there is no record whatsoever of his activities before the *Mayflower* landed in the New World. Nothing was written about him, as far as we know, until *Mourt's Relation*, a book written by Pilgrims William Bradford and Edward Winslow (the name "Mourt" is possibly a pen name or misprint of the name of the book's editor, George Morton), mentions Standish for the first time when he steps off the *Mayflower* on November 15, 1620.

It is not known where or even in which year Standish was born, much less on which day. There are clues and there are guesses, but very few hard facts. The closest thing to an original source referencing his birth and family came at the time of his death in 1656. Nathaniel

Morton, who knew Standish personally, wrote in *New England's Memorial*, "This year Capt. Miles Standish expired his mortal life. He was a gentleman, born in Lancashire, and was heir apparent unto a great estate of lands and livings, surreptitiously detained from him; his great grandfather being a second or younger brother from the house of Standish." This information about his lands and his grandfather is taken almost word for word from Standish's own will, thus calling into question how much Morton actually knew of Standish's personal history before the captain died. Still, this brief biography has led to a lot of speculation about his life before joining the Pilgrims, and about his family history.

THE CASE FOR DUXBURY

Differing opinions about where Standish was born have resulted in a debate of sorts that has played out over more than a century. One of the earliest attempts to settle the question was motivated by money. Based on the idea that certain estates in England had been secretly (or perhaps only sneakily) taken from Standish, a group of his American descendants got together in 1846 and hired an agent to try to recover those lands for them, his rightful heirs.

This agent was I. W. R. Bromley, Esq., and according to Justin Winsor in his 1849 book *History of the Town of Duxbury, Massachusetts*, the descendants paid him as much as $3,000 to conduct his investigation—a considerable sum in those days. Bromley used this money to set sail for England in November 1846. His destination was the town of Chorley, near Duxbury, where he hoped to search the parish registry for the entry recording the birth of Miles Standish. The Reverend Thomas Cruddas Porteus, in his essay "Some Recent Investigations Concerning the Ancestry of Capt. Myles Standish" in *The New England Historical and Genealogical Register* of 1914, says that the particular estates that the American descendants hoped to claim were in Duxbury Park.

ENGLAND IN THE LATE 1500s

When Miles Standish was born in or about 1584, England was at the height of the Elizabethan Period. The reign of Queen Elizabeth I lasted from 1558–1603, during which time England built itself into a commercial and naval power, having defeated the mighty Spanish Armada in 1588.

The year 1584—whether or not this was Standish's actual birth year—was a significant one. This was the year Prince William of Orange was assassinated, an event that led to England's increased involvement in the war between the Netherlands and Spain. It was also the year Sir Walter Raleigh received permission to explore and settle North America, leading to the eventual establishment of the Virginia colony of Roanoke. While the colony did not last, it was an important first step in England's pursuit of such colonies in America. Over the next few years, England's war with Spain grew, English explorers such as Raleigh and Sir Francis Drake sailed around the world, and William Shakespeare wrote some of the world's most famous plays.

As the sixteenth century came to a close and Standish grew toward adulthood, there were a few options available to young men seeking the title of "gentleman." In *Description of England*, William Harrison writes that "a captain in the wars . . . is able and will bear the port, charge, and countenance of a gentleman." Whether or not this was Standish's motivation in joining the military cannot be known, but his war service changed not only his life but the history of the New World.

Bromley was unable to prove any connection linking Miles Standish to Duxbury (besides the fact that a New England town founded by Standish and others was named "Duxbury"), but he

Queen Elizabeth I commissioned Sir Walter Raleigh (*above*) to establish an English colony in the New World. Raleigh, who had never traveled to America, created a plan to settle a specific area on the coast and named it Virginia. His first colony on Roanoke Island proved to be a failure when all of its inhabitants disappeared from the settlement.

claimed that his lack of success was due to foul play: In looking through the records in Chorley, he found that the pages where Miles's birth would have been recorded, had he been born in 1584, were heavily damaged to the point of being unreadable. Having read some of Bromley's letters to the group of descendants, Winsor became convinced that Bromley's story was true. Writing just a couple of years after Bromley's trip, he made the attorney's case for him, saying:

> The records were all readily deciphered, with the exception of the years 1584 and 1585, the very dates, about which time

Standish is supposed to have been born . . . and the conclusion was at once established, that it had been done purposely with pumice stone or otherwise, to destroy the legal evidence of the parentage of Standish, and his consequent title to the estates thereabout.

Bromley also implied that the rector of the parish, the official responsible for keeping the records, was in on the foul play. Once the rector figured out that Bromley was looking for Miles Standish's birth record to try to prove his ownership of the Duxbury estates, the rector "compelled him to pay the sum of about £15, or suffer imprisonment," in Winsor's telling. Years later, in 1888, John Abbot Goodwin elaborated on these facts in *The Pilgrim Republic*, stating that "the leaf for 1584-5, in the Chorley parish-register, had been pumiced so carefully as to leave no trace of the writing, though the record is otherwise complete from 1549 to 1652. . . . In 1847 Mr. Bromley, an attorney for the heirs, obtained leave as an antiquary to examine the volume, but the rector, finding him searching for Standish's birth, arrested him under some ancient law, and enforced on him a fine of about £75, with the alternative of imprisonment." Winsor concluded from Bromley's tale that "Standish was the true and rightful heir to the estates, and that they were truly 'surreptitiously detained' from him, and are now enjoyed by those, to whom they do not justly belong." Goodwin similarly believed that it was "quite evident that the legal proof of Standish's birth and descent has been destroyed to secure a fraudulent transfer of his inheritance." Seventy years later, however, Porteus would challenge Winsor's and Goodwin's conclusions.

THE CASE FOR ORMSKIRK OR ISLE OF MAN

In his 1920 book *Captain Myles Standish: His Lost Lands and Lancashire Connections*, Porteus goes through the Bromley story point by point and dismantles it. Porteus points out that at least one other person saw the registry and said that it had been worn down by dampness and overuse, but not intentionally damaged. In fact, Porteus asks, why would somebody take the time to carefully erase several months' worth of entries just to get rid of the record of Miles Standish's birth? He also points out that there were other gaps in the registry, some of them years long, disproving Winsor's and Goodwin's claims that the only gap was 1584–1585.

Next he takes aim at the story of the rector being in on the conspiracy. According to Porteus, Dr. Myles Standish, a descendant of Miles, said that the rector only threatened Bromley with a fine. The threat of imprisonment, Porteus said, was a figment of Goodwin's imagination. Furthermore, the "fine" was probably in fact a standard fee charged during those times for looking over the records.

Porteus then goes on to establish the case for Miles being linked not to Duxbury but to the town of Ormskirk, as well to as the Isle of Man. In 1912, Porteus happened upon a deed from 1529 mentioning a Margarete Standysshe islands in "Ormskirk, Borscoghe, Croston, Mawdisley, Wryghtington, [and] Newburghe." These are the same locations that Miles mentions in his will as the lands that were "detained" from him. The one exception is that the will also mentions the Isle of Man.

After he found this deed, Porteus's curiosity was aroused, and he continued his research. He then went on to find about 30 more deeds plus other references that let him establish that a whole line of Standishes had resided in Ormskirk, separate from the main line known to have lived in the town of Standish. Both towns, Ormskirk and Standish, are in the county of Lancashire, and the Ormskirk line of the Standish family originally descended from the Standish line of the Standish family, but Porteus says they separated as early as the 1400s. "Captain Myles Standish belonged to a branch of the Standishes that was settled from 1440, if not earlier, at Ormskirk," according to Porteus. "The six places in Lancashire to which Captain Myles refers in his will were the places in which the Standishes of this branch held land, and they seem to have held nowhere else. A clinching bit of evidence is found in the fact that some members of this branch settled in the Isle of Man."

Next Porteus describes the Standish family history in Ormskirk, beginning with William Standish (first mentioned in lawsuits in 1444 and 1446), and the addition of the lands in the other locations over the next several generations. Porteus thus proves that all of the lands except those on the Isle of Man were in the Ormskirk Standish family before Miles was born. Given that Miles claimed he was heir to all these lands, this would seem to make a strong case for Miles Standish being from the Ormskirk line—in which case he would have been born in Ormskirk. Porteus, however, was not able to find any record of his birth in the Ormskirk parish registers, either. Those records, like the Chorley ones, were damaged, so it's still possible Miles was born there, but there's no direct proof.

Porteus mentions another and perhaps stronger possibility, though. Around 1566, William's direct descendant Hugh Standish inherited all the lands in the Ormskirk Standish family and then started selling them off. In the record of one of those transactions, Porteus discovered that there was a relative of Hugh named John Standish who lived on the Isle of Man. Other historians already knew about a branch of the Standish family on Man, but Porteus directly links that line to Ormskirk, and thus provides an explanation for Miles being able to claim to be the heir of both the lands held by the Ormskirk Standishes as well as lands on the Isle of Man.

The records on the Isle of Man are generally incomplete and unreliable, however, so once again there is no record of Miles being born there. So while Porteus does not claim it to be fact, his conclusion is that Miles is most likely the descendant of the Standish line on the Isle of Man. Another historian, George V. C. Young, argues in his

1984 book *Pilgrim Myles Standish, First Manx American* that Miles was in fact born on the Isle of Man. Porteus leaves open the possibility, though, that Miles's father or perhaps grandfather returned from the Isle of Man to Lancashire, and that Nathaniel Morton was correct in saying that Miles was born there.

THE CASE FOR "WHO KNOWS?"

Later in the twentieth century, another person conducted some research into the mysterious case of Miles Standish's birth, and remained unconvinced by Porteus's arguments. This was Helen Moorwood, an amateur historian who started looking into Miles Standish while researching the history of Duxbury. In her essay "Pilgrim Father Captain Myles Standish of Duxbury Lancashire and Massachusetts," which appeared in the *Lancashire History Quarterly*, Moorwood recaps Porteus's theory of Miles being descended from the Standish family of Ormskirk and the Isle of Man, then states definitively, "The theory is wrong."

She also calls Young's theory of Miles being born on the Isle of Man "flawed." In fact, she says, Miles had no connection to the Isle of Man at all. How to explain the mention of that location in the will? "The 'Isle of Man' at the end of Myles' list was almost certainly the one in Croston, Lancashire, owned jointly by Standish in the [thirteenth century] and [fourteenth century]," says Moorwood.

In this article she claims to solve "most of the mysteries surrounding Myles," and states "that he was definitely a Standish of Duxbury and Standish," and thus indeed the rightful heir to the lands in Duxbury as his American descendants claimed. As for the actual place of his birth, however, she is less certain, saying only that he was born "in West Lancashire, probably in one of the six townships named in his Will."

To date, the last word in the long debate belongs to Dr. Jeremy Bangs, a historian and director of the Leiden American Pilgrim

Many historians have scoured old registers and ancient town registries in hopes of determining the location of Standish's birth, but there is no definitive answer. Dr. Jeremy Bangs (*above*) of the Leiden American Pilgrim Museum in the Netherlands believes that information from Standish's time is too incomplete to solve the mystery.

Museum who, in 2008, published "Myles Standish, Born Where? The State of the Question" on the Web site www.sail1620.org. In it, he takes Moorwood to task for what he calls her "masterpieces of obscurantism, comprising travesties of historical method." He goes on to say:

> Typically she announces what is to be proven in a later part. . . . The text of the document, she assures the reader, will be published at some future date. In the later part of the article, or in subsequent articles, if the subject comes up again, she

states that in the previous part, or in her earlier publication, she has more than sufficiently demonstrated her hypothesis to be true. . . . But nothing beyond the first announcement can be discovered.

For instance, Moorwood brings up the question of Miles Standish's ancestry, then says, "The answer (already given in the last article, with sources of the proof) is that he was definitely a Standish of Duxbury and Standish." Bangs says to this, "Despite the promise and the claims, no proof had been given in the preceding parts of the article."

Bangs also shoots down her theory about the Isle of Man mentioned in Miles's will being the Isle of Man Farm in Lancashire, pointing out that the name "Isle of Man" for that piece of land does not show up on any maps until 1848, and that there's no proof that any Standish family line owned that piece of property in the sixteenth century. He goes on to counter most of her other arguments, including a key one about Miles's ancestry. "The 1655 document that is the key evidence in Moorwood's claims to have revealed Myles Standish's genealogy," Bangs writes, "does not refer to the lands mentioned in Myles Standish's will, dated 1656. Moorwood thinks that Myles Standish's most important inheritance was Duxbury Hall and associated lands as specified in this document, although Myles does not name them in his will or any other document."

Not to say that Bangs is as convinced as Porteus or especially as Young of the Isle of Man connection. He writes, "Even if new evidence could be considered consistent with the argument, the demonstration would still indicate nothing more than a possibility." Bangs leaves open the possibility that Standish was born on the Isle of Man, but also that his family might have been from Lancashire and he born somewhere else, perhaps at a time when his mother was visiting friends or family.

Bangs's conclusion is more uncertain than those of most preceding historians. "Documentary evidence about the Standish families of Standish, Duxbury, Ormskirk, and the Isle of Man is extensive but incomplete," he says, continuing:

> . . . especially incomplete with regard to sources for genealogical information (baptisms, marriages, burials). Attempts to define his genealogical relation to earlier generations have not been successful, although T. R. [*sic*] Porteus succeeded in finding the Manx-Lancashire branch of the Standish family to which Myles somehow must have belonged. The only information we have about where Myles Standish was born is the ambiguous indication from his will.

The question of where Miles Standish was born must remain, for now, a mystery.

3

A Hired Gun

If Miles Standish's family history and birth are mysteries, the rest of his life before meeting up with the Pilgrims is not much clearer. T. C. Porteus in *Captain Myles Standish: His Lost Lands and Lancashire Connections* reports that some of Standish's descendants in the nineteenth century claimed to have seen documentation appointing him to the rank of lieutenant in the service of Queen Elizabeth, who died in 1603, and that the documentation said he was born in 1584. However, the documentation has never been found, so those details cannot be verified.

In *New England's Memorial*, Nathaniel Morton writes, "In his younger time he went over into the low countries, and was a soldier there, and came acquainted with the church at Leyden." During his service in the Low Countries, Standish must have served under the English commander Sir Horace Vere. In "Myles

Standish, Born Where?" Bangs points out that Vere led the only English regiment that served in the Low Countries, and that regiment recruited in Lancashire and the Isle of Man, each of which has been named as Standish's possible birthplace. This service would have given Standish not only formal military training, but actual combat experience. As captain, he would have been responsible for leading the men serving under him, drilling them, preparing them for war, then commanding them in battle. All this experience would prove essential to his role as the military commander of a settlement surrounded by hostile native forces.

As with most details of his early life, there is no record of Miles Standish having served in the Low Countries. Porteus says he "searched several volumes of the State Papers, Holland, in the Public Records Office, for any mention of him," but could find nothing. Records at a hospital in Leiden, Holland, list among its patients in 1601 a wounded soldier named Myls Stansen. Dr. Bangs and others believe this was Miles Standish. In fact, Bangs's own translation of a December 14, 2000 article in Holland's NRC-Handelsblad newspaper describes his efforts to save that hospital as a Pilgrim heritage site.

WHO WERE THE PILGRIMS?

The war between Spain and the Netherlands came to a halt in 1609 with a truce that was to last 12 years. A year earlier, a group of Pilgrims from the English town of Scrooby made their way to Holland on a short but dangerous boat journey. They were refugees, and were fleeing an environment that had become increasingly hostile to their religious views.

For decades England had alternated between Catholic and Protestant rulers. In 1559, the Protestant Queen Elizabeth I tried to unite all of her subjects under the Act of Uniformity, in which she declared that everybody must attend church every Sunday, and

WAR IN THE LOW COUNTRIES

In the late 1500s, the Low Countries—roughly the same area known today as "Benelux," short for Belgium, the Netherlands, and Luxembourg—were ruled by Spain, and the tales of cruelty at the hands of the Spanish governors aroused great sympathy in England for the people of that region. In 1579, several provinces in the Netherlands signed the Union of Utrecht, and two years later they declared their independence from Spain.

The sympathy among the English for the Netherlands grew as the war raged on over the years after the declaration of independence, but Spain was at the time the most powerful nation on Earth, so entering the war was no easy decision for Queen Elizabeth I of England. A series of assassinations and attacks by the Spanish, however, led the Queen to formally support the Netherlands in 1585. There were also religious reasons for her sympathies: The Netherlands, like England, was Protestant, and Spain was Catholic.

Englishmen were already fighting the Spanish in the Low Countries before 1585, but only as volunteers under Dutch command. The force that Queen Elizabeth sent over consisted of trained soldiers under English command.

Declaring her reasons for sending the troops, Queen Elizabeth noted the bloody rule of the Spanish and the right of the Dutch people to rise up and win their freedom. It was much the same language that the Founding Fathers of America would use nearly 200 years later in declaring independence from England.

that those church services must follow the rules of the Church of England. There were groups of people, however, who believed that everyone should be able to interpret the Bible the way he or she saw fit. These people were known as Separatists, and there were many different but unconnected Separatist congregations all across England. They believed that congregations were independent units that could elect their own officials, including their pastor and elder, and that no higher ruler—whether it be a bishop, the pope, or a king or queen—could pick their leaders for them or tell them how to read the Bible. In this regard, they were similar to the Puritans with one key difference: Although the Puritans hoped to stay in the Church of England and reform it, the Separatists felt the Church was beyond saving. Thus, they sought to remove themselves from it altogether.

The Separatist congregation in Scrooby was headed by their pastor Richard Clifton, with John Robinson as his assistant. Their fellow Cambridge University graduate William Brewster was a member of their congregation, as was a young William Bradford. The congregation held meetings at the Scrooby manor house, where Brewster's father had been the caretaker.

Queen Elizabeth died in 1603 and was succeeded by King James I. It was unclear at first what religious policies the king might adopt. Any hope that the Separatists had of greater religious freedom, however, was soon dashed when King James spoke at the Conference of Hampton Court in 1604. As quoted by John S. C. Abbott in *Miles Standish, the Puritan Capitan*, the king said, "I will have one doctrine, one discipline, one religion. And I will make you conform or I will harry you out of this land or else worse." If the king was threatening to force the Puritans, who remained part of the Church of England, to conform, then the Separatists could not expect any lighter treatment.

Even before this, things had been getting dangerous for Separatists. In *The Pilgrim Republic*, John Abbot Goodwin writes, "Governor Bradford refers to a printed list of some eighteen Separatists dying of jail-fever in London between 1586 and 1592; he adds that many died from the hardships of their prisons." Three prominent leaders were hanged in 1593. Over the years, harassment and arrests of Separatists grew. The congregation at Scrooby was not formed until 1606,

Queen Elizabeth I and her successor, King James I (*above*), believed all of their subjects should conform to the Church of England and persecuted those who did not adhere to the same beliefs. The Puritans and the Separatists, two similar groups who wanted more religious freedom, were harassed, imprisoned, and executed until they joined the Church or left the country.

by which time the atmosphere had grown very grim. In *Of Plymouth Plantation*, William Bradford tells of the increasingly unbearable situation in which they lived: ". . . they could not long continue in any peaceable condition, but were hunted and persecuted on every side, so as their former afflictions were but as flea-bitings in comparison of these which now came upon them. For some were taken and clapped up in prison, others had their houses beset and watched night and day, and hardly escaped their hands." The time had come to leave England.

ON TO HOLLAND

Even before the 12-year truce between Spain and the Netherlands was signed in 1609, the Low Countries were still a safer place than England for the Separatists. Article 13 of the Union of Utrecht proclaimed that "each person shall remain free, especially in his religion, and that no one shall be persecuted or investigated because of their religion." Not only was there greater freedom to worship as one wished in the Netherlands, there was also more freedom of the press. Francis Dillon, in his book *The Pilgrims*, explains that this was important to the Separatists because "Most other countries had a strict censorship. Puritan books and pamphlets were burned in England but freely published in Holland."

Despite King James's threats to run religious nonconformists out of England, he did not make it easy for them to leave. Laws were passed making it illegal to leave the country without permission from the government, and it seemed that the government would rather throw the Separatists in jail than let them leave. Law enforcement officials patrolled the seaports looking for people trying to flee the country. The Scrooby congregation thus had to make secret plans to get to Holland. In the autumn of 1607, they arranged for a ship to take them at great expense from the port town of Boston to their new home.

Unfortunately they were too trusting, and the captain of the ship, once he had received his money, turned them over to the port's law officers. Abbot gives a vivid description of what happened next in *Miles Standish, the Puritan Capitan*: "Rudely they were seized, their trunks broken open, their clothing confiscated, and even the persons of their women searched with cruel indelicacy. Thus plundered and outraged they were placed in open boats and taken to the shore, where they were exhibited to the derisive gaze and the jeers of an ignorant and a brutal populace. . . . After gloomy incarceration for a month, Mr. Brewster and six others of the most prominent men were bound over for trial, and the rest were released, woe-stricken, sick and impoverished, to find their way back, as best they could, to the Scrooby which they had left, and where they no longer had any homes. Oh man! what a fiend hast thou been in the treatment of thy brother man!"

Yet their spirits were not broken. The very next spring, in 1608, they tried again, this time hiring a Dutch captain and departing not from a seaport but from an unpopulated strip of coastline near the Humber River. The women and children sailed down the river in a small boat known as a bark, while the men traveled overland. Stormy seas, however, forced the bark to take shelter in a small creek. The bark became grounded, and so they had to wait until the next day for the tide to rise and the ship to arrive before they could try again.

In the morning they had only gotten one boatload of men to the ship when the Dutch captain spotted the approach of armed law officers. Immediately he set sail, leaving mostly women and children behind but some men as well. The men on the ship pleaded with him to return to shore and not leave their wives and children behind, but the captain would not risk it, for he too would have been subject to arrest and fines if he had been caught. So they sailed on. After more stormy seas and a terrible crossing, the ship eventually reached Amsterdam 14 days later.

All of those left behind on the coast were captured. Some men escaped, but others, including John Robinson, William Brewster, and William Bradford, stayed with the women and children to help them as they could. While the illegal emigrants were again treated roughly at first, the authorities weren't sure what to do with them. As Kate Caffrey writes in *The Mayflower*, the authorities "finally decided that it was unreasonable to punish [the women] for merely doing their Christian duty—obeying their husbands. They could not be sent home, for they had no homes to go to; the only solution was to pack them off to Amsterdam." At long last, the members of the Scrooby congregation who had dared make the journey were together in Holland.

THE PILGRIMS' TIME IN LEIDEN

While Holland offered the Separatists the religious freedom they wanted, Amsterdam didn't end up working out for them. There were already some Separatists from England in Amsterdam at the time— one group had come over in 1593 following the arrest of their minister and some congregation members. In 1608 there was trouble brewing within the Ancient Church, as this original group of religious refugees had come to be known, and the group from Scrooby worried about getting caught up in it. William Bradford writes, "the flames of contention were like to break out in that ancient church itself . . . which things they prudently foreseeing thought it was best to remove before they were any way engaged with the same."

The place they chose to remove themselves to was the city of Leiden (or "Leyden"), about 25 miles (40.2 kilometers) to the southeast. Their leader, John Clifton, decided to stay behind in Amsterdam and join the Ancient Church, and John Robinson became their new minister. They settled down there and mixed as well as they could into their new surroundings.

After more than a decade in their new home, they decided it was once again time to move on. In *Of Plymouth Plantation*, Bradford lists four reasons for this. The first was the worry that the hardships they faced in Holland would dissuade others in England from joining them, and make it difficult to keep those that did arrive. It's true that Separatists found work in Leiden, but their jobs were not highpaying, so their standard of living was low. There was also the language barrier to consider, and the feeling associated with being an exile in a foreign land.

The second reason was the fact that the hardships were weighing heavily upon those that were already in Leiden. As Bradford writes, "the people generally bore all these difficulties very cheerfully and with a resolute courage . . . yet old age began to steal on many of them." Some were getting old before their time, he said, and he expected that within a few years many would start to scatter, either because they'd grown weary of the hard work or for other reasons.

Concern for the children of the congregation was the third reason for the Separatists' decision to relocate. The hard work took an especially big toll on the group's youngest members, so that "their bodies bowed under the weight . . . and became decrepit in their early youth," according to Bradford. Even worse in Bradford's mind were the many temptations that Leiden had to offer young people. Bradford says the children were "drawn away by evil examples into extravagant and dangerous courses, getting the reins off their necks and departing from their parents. Some became soldiers, others took upon them far voyages by sea, and others some worse courses tending to dissoluteness and the danger of their souls, to the great grief of their parents and the dishonor of God."

Finally, the Separatists wished to leave Holland in order to spread the word of Christ to remote parts of the world. Their primary focus was America, which Bradford describes as "being devoid of all civil inhabitants, where there are only savage and brutish men which

Although King James I vowed to run the nonconformists out of England, the government passed several laws preventing citizens from leaving without permission. Separatists, hoping to immigrate to Holland, were frequently arrested and sent to jail for trying to flee the country.

range up and down, little otherwise than the wild beasts of the same." Despite this low assessment, these were the people the Separatists hoped to convert to Christianity.

Nathaniel Morton gives a fifth reason for the Separatists leaving Holland. Within a few generations, the descendants of the Separatists would lose their "Englishness" and become Dutch, he wrote in

New England's Memorial. Despite the fact that they had been more or less run out of their country, they were still patriotic Englishmen and Englishwomen. By building a home in a new land, they would be able to remain English, as would their children and their children's children.

Bradford also offers another motive in addition to the four he spells out explicitly: the possibility of war returning to Holland. The 12-year truce with Spain was set to expire in 1620, and the Thirty Year's War (as it would come to be known) had already broken out between Catholics and Protestants in 1618. "The Spaniard might prove as cruel as the savages of America," Bradford writes, "and the famine and pestilence as sore here as there." John Robinson's Leiden congregation thus made the decision to try their luck in America.

Many in the Leiden congregation were naturally fearful. Though the opportunity to convert the native people to Christianity was appealing, a good number of them feared being in "continual danger of the savage people, who are cruel, barbarous and most treacherous, being most furious in their rage and merciless where they overcome; not being content only to kill and take away life, but delight to torment men in the most bloody manner that may be," as Bradford puts it. The graphic examples of torments he describes offer insight into the mentality of the Separatists embarking on the trip. Such fears drove the desire to have a strong military man among them to defend the group from the "savages."

STANDISH VS. SMITH

That man, of course, would be Miles Standish. Following the signing of the 12-year truce in 1609, Standish decided not to return to his native England but to instead stay in Leiden. While there, it appears that he met and got to know the pastor of the Separatist congregation, John Robinson. The best indication of this is Robinson's letter to Bradford, written in 1623, in which he refers to Standish as "your Captain, whom I love, and am persuaded the Lord in great mercy and for much good hath sent you him, if you use him aright. He is a man humble and meek amongst you, and towards all in ordinary course." In his essay "Miles Standish, Born Where?" Jeremy Bangs writes:

> This evidence of obviously personal acquaintance alone is enough to indicate that the Pilgrims' contact with Standish began in Leiden, but in addition there is a silver cup inscribed, apparently authentically, as a gift from Robinson to Standish; and there is the final circumstance that Standish left a legacy to John Robinson's granddaughter "Marcye Robenson whome I tenderly love for her Grandfathers sacke." Only in Leiden could Robinson have met Standish; and only in Leiden could Standish have formed such an attachment to Robinson.

Standish might not have been the Separatists' first choice for the assignment. While in London their agents contacted Captain John Smith, famous for his explorations in 1614 of the area that he named New England. The Separatists considered him too expensive, though, according to Smith's own account, and thought they could get by without his knowledge of the area and instead just bring the detailed map he had made of New England. Captain Smith's fame also worked against him. As Nathaniel Philbrick puts it in *Mayflower*, "Smith's fatal flaw, as far as the Pilgrims were concerned, was that he knew too much. In the beginning of the settlement, they would have had no choice but to do as he said, and this could be dangerous. Smith possessed a strong personality, and a man of his worldly nature might come to dominate what they intended to be an inherently religious enclave." Standish might not know nearly as much about America as Smith, but there would be much less risk of him taking control of the colony.

There is no record of the meetings between Standish and Robinson or any other members of the church that led to his signing on for the journey, but it is clear from Bradford's descriptions of the natives that he and the other Separatists knew they would be trying to settle in hostile territory and would need good defenses. There were no other military men among them, a testament to just how much faith they put in Standish's abilities as a military leader. They would not have to wait long after reaching the New World to find out whether they had made the right choice.

4

The Voyage
of the *Mayflower*

Although nothing is known of how Standish spent the years between the end of the Dutch-Spanish war and the time the Separatists decided to leave Leiden, the goings-on of the congregation are fairly well documented for this time period, particularly in the lead-up to their 1620 voyage. Before they could leave Leiden, the Separatists still needed to work out a couple of details—for instance, where were they going? Many of the congregation's members wanted to go to Guiana, which Sir Walter Raleigh had written about in glowing terms after exploring up the Orinoco River. The region's "perpetual spring," as William Bradford put it in *Of Plymouth Plantation*, would mean they would need less clothing and provisions. Others were in favor of going to Virginia, due to the success (moderate as it was) of the English in Jamestown.

There were also arguments against each of these locations. The fear with Guiana was that being a hot country, it would expose the settlers to diseases unfamiliar to them. They also worried that the Spanish who controlled the area would eventually drive them out. As for Virginia, the English who settled Jamestown were not Separatists, so the possibility that they would face religious persecution there just as they did in England still existed.

Utlimately, the argument in favor of Virginia proved to win out over the others, though the Separatists were banking on the hope that they could live there under the Government of Virginia with a grant of religious feedom by King James I. In 1617, the congregation sent two members, John Carver and Robert Cushman, as representatives to England to try to secure this freedom, as well as to talk to the First (London) Virginia Company, the group that controlled the land from approximately what is today Cape Fear, North Carolina, to Long Island Sound, about securing a patent—that is, an official grant to start a colony.

They did not manage to get an official document from the king guaranteeing freedom of religion, but James did promise that he would not bother them as long as they "carried themselves peaceably." This was enough for many of the Separatists, as even an official document could be revoked at any time and thus did not offer much more protection than the king's promise. Carver and Cushman did, however, obtain a patent from the Virginia Company. The company was eager to work with them for the same reason King James was willing to grant them religious freedom in the New World that he would not have granted them in England—they wanted a greater English presence in the Americas. Nathaniel Philbrick wrote in *Mayflower*, "it had become apparent that the colonization of North America was essential to England's future prosperity. France, Holland, and especially Spain had already taken advantage of the seemingly limitless resources of the New World." For James, colonization was a matter of competition with the other European powers. For the Virginia Company, it was a matter of self-enrichment. By June 1619, Carver and Cushman had a patent in hand for a tract of land at the northern end of the Virginia territory, according to John Abbot Goodwin in *The Pilgrim Republic*.

The Separatists now had a destination. What they did not yet have was funding, and the Virginia Company was too broke to provide them with transportation to America. They talked to a Dutch group known as the New Netherlands Company, but broke off negotiations after a London businessman named Thomas Weston approached them with an offer. His group, known as Merchant Adventurers, consisted of businessmen who wished to finance a colony in the New World with the hope of making money from it. George F. Willison says of these businessmen in his book *Saints and Strangers*, "With scarcely an exception they were induced to risk their money solely by hope of large and quick profits. They were simply not interested in the Separatists as such, having no desire whatever to establish the Holy Discipline in the New World." For their part, the Separatists were just thankful for the financing needed to get them to their new home.

After the congregation and the Merchant Adventurers struck a deal, the Second (Plymouth) Virginia Company got permission to control the northern portion of the original Virginia lands and renamed it "New England." The Separatists thus began a new debate about where they should go, and decided on New England. Separated from the Virginian government to the south, they could enjoy greater freedom of religion. Weston wanted them to go to New England, too, thinking that the settlers could make a profit from the good fishing in the area. But the decision to go to New England caused some of the Separatists to back out of the trip, and then the group found out that they could not get exclusive rights to fish the area. Finally they made up their minds—they would head for "some place about Hudson's River for their habitation," as Bradford wrote in *Of Plymouth Plantation*.

To complicate matters again, Weston changed the terms of the agreement, upsetting many of the Separatists. Carver and Cushman, meanwhile, said they had no choice but to accept the new terms. The Merchant Adventurers also insisted that some non-Separatists take the place of those who had backed out. Worse yet, in June 1620, as everybody was making arrangements to leave, Weston had still not found a ship to take them to America. The Separatists had great faith, however, and still believed they would get to the New World.

Finally, transportation was secured. The Leiden congregation bought a small ship called the *Speedwell*, a 60-ton (54.4-metric ton) vessel that would take some of the party across the Atlantic and stay there for "fishing and such affairs as might be for the good and benefit of the colony," says Bradford. Weston came through with a 180-ton (163.2-metric ton) ship in London. This was the *Mayflower*, "a fine ship," according to a quote from Cushman found in Willison's *Saints and Strangers*. This was lucky for the soon-to-be settlers, as the *Speedwell* would turn out not to be a fine ship.

FALSE STARTS

In describing the Separatists' departure from Leiden, Bradford says, "So they left that goodly and pleasant city which had been their resting place near twelve years; but they knew they were pilgrims, and looked not much on those things, but lift up their eyes to the heavens." This is the first time that anybody used the word "pilgrims" to describe this group of immigrants to America. However, after that they never referred to themselves by this name, but instead called themselves "Saints," in the sense of "God's chosen people." Francis Dillon explains in *The Pilgrims*, "The Plymouth Separatists were not called the Pilgrims until the 1790s, when the Reverend Robbins in

While many English Separatists were satisfied to settle in Holland, there were some who grew unhappy with their new home. Looking toward the future, Separatist leaders such as William Bradford believed establishing an English colony in America would allow them to practice their religious beliefs, maintain their patriotism, and spread Christianity.

a sermon on Forefathers' Day quoted the pilgrim reference . . . and thereafter they were Pilgrims." While it's debatable whether Miles Standish ever actually joined the Separatist church, he is still counted among the Pilgrims.

On July 22, 1620, those of the Leiden congregation who decided to make the journey—just 46 out of a total of 300—prepared to set sail from Delfthaven, Holland, aboard the *Speedwell*. Many were leaving friends and family behind—in some cases wives and children—loved ones they realized they might never see again. Bradford reports that "truly doleful was the sight of that sad and mournful parting, to see what sighs and sobs and prayers did sound amongst them, what tears did gush from every eye, and pithy speeches pierced each heart." Pastor John Robinson, who had decided to stay behind in Leiden, led some prayers and gave a farewell speech to those departing. In the New World William Brewster would serve as the congregation's spiritual leader.

The Pilgrims, as they are now known, had an easy sail to Southampton, England, where they met up with the *Mayflower*, which had sailed from London. Miles Standish was a soldier in the Netherlands and knew Robinson—if he did indeed stay on in Leiden after the war with Spain ended, he would have been aboard the *Speedwell* as it made its way from Holland to England, though there is no direct proof of this. With him was his wife, Rose, whose background also is a mystery to historians. Just as researchers have combed records looking for mention of Standish's birth, so too have they searched for any documentation of his marriage to Rose, but here, too, they have come up empty.

The trip to Southampton proved to be the last smooth sailing the Pilgrims would enjoy. On August 5, 1620, they at long last departed for their trip across the Atlantic. After just a few days, however, they discovered that the *Speedwell* was as "leaky as a sieve," as one of the travelers, Robert Cushman, wrote in a letter to a friend. They had to turn back. They put in at Dartmouth harbor and had repairs made. The wind turned against them, however, and they were stuck in Dartmouth. They were eating through their food supplies and didn't have funds to buy more. They began to fear they would run out before they got to America. They were also aware of the disastrous trip made by another group of Separatists a couple of years earlier from Holland to Virginia, during which 130 of the 180 people aboard died from diseases and lack of fresh water. No doubt all these things weighed on the minds of those aboard the *Speedwell* and the *Mayflower*, many of whom wanted to call off the voyage altogether.

In his letter, Cushman wrote, "Friend, if ever we make a plantation, God works a miracle."

The ship appeared to be in good shape when they again set sail on August 23. Once again, however, it was not to be. The *Speedwell* sprung more leaks, and they had to return to England once more, this time to the port of Plymouth. (The area where they would land in the New World was already called "Plimouth" at this time, so it is just a coincidence that the harbor they would finally leave from shared the same name.) This time, there would be no fixing the ship. Despite the money they had put into purchasing and mending it, and the plans they had for using it as a fishing vessel in America, the Pilgrims had to abandon the ship. Some of the party, including Cushman, decided that they had had enough and would stay in England. The rest crowded aboard the *Mayflower*—102 passengers in all—and tried their luck once more. They left Plymouth on September 6, and this time there would be no turning back.

ROUGH SEAS

Despite spending more than two months crossing the ocean, William Bradford only writes a couple of paragraphs about the voyage in *Of Plymouth Plantation*. When they set sail from Plymouth they had "a prosperous wind." For the first part of the trip they had good weather, which would have allowed Miles Standish to conduct military-style drills with some of the other colonists in preparation for forming a militia in the New World. Thomas J. Fleming in *One Small Candle* describes some of these exercises, such as drills with swords. More important than learning how to handle a sword, though, "was instruction in handling the cumbersome matchlock muskets of 1620. . . . Firing a matchlock was slow work. Again and again, Standish had his men go through the lengthy maneuver on the *Mayflower's* unsteady deck." Firing the muskets would have created a lot of smoke and noise as well as wasted gunpowder, so "Standish probably had the men go through the monotonous drill more often than he had them fire," Fleming says.

The trip was not without its troubles, however. First, there was the usual seasickness that strikes those not used to being on an ocean-going ship, even in good weather. As if that weren't bad enough, there was one sailor in particular who teased those that got sick. Bradford said this man was constantly cursing them, and told them that "he hoped to help cast half of them overboard before they came to their journey's end."

As fate would have it, this sailor would be the first one to die on the voyage. Bradford describes the incident, which he calls "a special work of God's providence," with a bit of gloating in his voice: "But it pleased God before they came half seas over, to smite this young man with a grievous disease, of which he died in a desperate manner, and so was himself the first that was thrown overboard. Thus his curses light on his own head, and it was an astonishment to all his fellows for they noted it to be the just hand of God upon him."

Soon after this they would encounter many storms and rough seas. Some of the storms were so fierce that they had to take in all the sails and wait until the winds died down, sometimes days at a time. One storm was so strong it cracked one of the *Mayflower's* main beams. This started a discussion among many of the ship's crew and passengers as to whether they should turn back, even though they were almost halfway to America. They were able to repair the beam, however, and caulk some leaky spots in the deck and upper works. As they continued their trip, the beam held up, even through more storms.

Amazingly, only one other person besides the ill-tempered sailor would die during the voyage. This was William Butten, a servant to Dr. Samuel Fuller of the Leiden congregation. The cause of his death was not recorded, but he was buried at sea on November 7. Just two days later, one of the *Mayflower* crew cried, "Land ho!"

Upon the sight of land, the passengers and crew "were not a little joyful," Bradford says. Unfortunately, the land they saw was Cape Cod; they had sailed too far north. They set sail south for the mouth of the Hudson, but they soon encountered the dangerous shoals (raised sandy areas in shallow water) of Pollack Rip. Once again the *Mayflower* would have to turn back. With the people on board showing signs of disease, the wind turning against them, and the Hudson 250 miles (402.3 km) away, Captain Christopher Jones of the *Mayflower* decided that they would return to Cape Cod and set anchor there.

THE FIRST EXPLORATORY EXPEDITION

The ship made its way back safely and set anchor in Cape Cod Harbor, today known as Provincetown Harbor, at the tip of the cape. Before the travelers could set foot on land, however, there was some business to which they needed to attend. Because they were now going to settle in New England but their patent was for Virginia, there would be no government ruling them. Thus, they decided it was necessary to form their own government. Given that about half the settlers were Saints (Separatists from the Leiden congregation) and the others were not, this was especially important. The result was the Mayflower Compact, a short document written on the ship that basically said the men (women were considered little more than property of the men) agreed to form a government that would set laws, elect officers, and more, and that everybody must obey these laws. On November 11, most of the men signed the compact. While they acknowledged themselves to be subjects of King James, the agreement to which they signed their names also established a form of democracy that would be an inspiration to the Founding Fathers.

THE MAYFLOWER COMPACT

Miles Standish was the sixth of 41 men on the *Mayflower* to sign the historic Mayflower Compact. Here is the text in its entirety:

In the name of God, amen. We whose names are underwritten, tho loyal subjects of our dread sovereign Lord, King James, by the grace of God, of Great Britain, France, and Ireland, King, Defender of the faith, etc. Having undertaken for the glory of God, and advancement of the Christian faith, and the honor of our King and country, a voyage to plant the first colony in the northern parts of Virginia; do by these presents solemnly and mutually, in the presence of God and one another, covenant and combine ourselves together into a civil body politic, for our better ordering and preservation, and furtherance of the ends aforesaid; and by virtue hereof, do enact, constitute, and frame such just and equal laws, ordinances, acts, constitutions, and officers, from time to time, as shall be thought most meet and convenient for the general good of the colony; unto which we promise all due submission and obedience. In witness whereof, we have hereunto subscribed our names, at Cape Cod, the eleventh of November, in the reign of our sovereign Lord King James, of England, France, and Ireland, the eighteenth, and of Scotland the fifty-fourth, Anno Dom. 1620

With the Mayflower Compact signed, the settlers chose John Carver to be their governor up until their next New Year's Day (March 25, according to the calendar used at that time). They were ready to send the first people ashore. Sixteen well-armed men stepped off the *Mayflower* and into the New World. Bradford writes, "Being thus arrived in a good harbor, and brought safe to land, they fell upon their knees and blessed the God of Heaven." While Standish is not mentioned at this point in *Of Plymouth Plantation* or *Mourt's Relation*, historians such as J. S. C. Abbott believe that, as the military captain, he led this first trip ashore. It was a short visit, lasting just from afternoon to early evening, and a disappointing one. They found no fresh water, heavily wooded land, and no local inhabitants. They did, however, find some red cedar which they burned upon the ship, thus providing not just warmth but a means of helping get rid of the terrible smell from so many people not having bathed in more than two months.

Several days later, the first real exploratory expedition took place. The plan was to explore by shallop, a large boat that can either be rowed or set with a sail. In order to fit the shallop on the *Mayflower*, the settlers had taken the boat apart and stored it in four pieces below deck. They hauled the pieces onto land on November 13 and the carpenter set to work putting the boat back together. He made slow progress, however, and many grew impatient. They decided to explore the surrounding area by walking overland instead.

It is at this point that Miles Standish steps into history, his name recorded for the first time in *Mourt's Relation*. On November 15, 1620, "with cautions, directions, and instructions, sixteen men were set out with every man his musket, sword, and corslet [a type of body armor], under the conduct of Captain Miles Standish."

It was a dangerous undertaking. They still did not know if they would meet any of the region's native people, and if they did, whether they would be friendly or hostile. They also had to make do with whatever they could carry, so they wouldn't have much food or ammunition with them. Standish had them march in single file along the seaside. After only a mile (1.6 km), they saw their first Native Americans. At first they thought the people were Captain Jones and some of the *Mayflower* crew along with the ship's dog—until they saw the men turn and run into the woods.

When rough waters prevented them from sailing to Virginia, members of the Leiden congregation decided to stay in New England. Without a royal patent for this location, these Pilgrims drafted and signed their own declaration of self-government, called the Mayflower Compact. Above, signatures on the Mayflower Compact.

At this point, many people would have turned back to report what they had seen. Captain Standish instead ordered his men to pursue the Native Americans into the woods, "partly to see if they could speak with them, and partly to discover if there might not be more of them lying in ambush," Bradford writes. They followed as best they could, but the natives were too fast for them. By looking at their footprints the Pilgrims could tell that the natives stopped at the top of a hill to see if they were still being followed. The Pilgrims followed the natives' tracks for miles but finally had to give up as night came on. They built a fire and took turns keeping watch throughout the night, three men to a shift.

The next morning they followed the tracks again but found no sign of any Native American villages. Later that morning they finally found fresh water, a spring from which they drank "our first New England water with as much delight as ever we drank drink in all our lives," according to *Mourt's Relation*.

After resting and drinking they went to the shoreline and built a fire as a signal to let their comrades on the *Mayflower* know where they were and that they were safe. They continued on and found mounds of sand. One in particular aroused their curiosity—it was covered with grass mats, and had a wooden structure on top and an earthen pot on one end. They dug into this mound and found a bow and some rotten arrows—they had accidentally dug into a grave. They returned the bow and arrows and restored the grave as best they could.

Next they found an old iron kettle, evidence that they were not the first Europeans to set foot here. The kettle could have been from a French shipwreck a few years earlier, as Nathaniel Philbrick suggests in *Mayflower*, or perhaps it was left behind by English or Breton fisherman, according to George F. Willison in *Saints and Strangers*, or stolen from a ship by the Native Americans, says Dillon in *The Pilgrims*. In this same area they found another sand mound. This one was not covered in mats. In fact, the sand still showed handprints from when the Native Americans patted it down. The Pilgrims dug into this mound and found a basket with bushels of corn.

With their food supplies aboard the *Mayflower* running dangerously low, they decided they would have to steal the corn. Standish had some of the men stand guard in a ring around the mound as others loaded as much as they could in the kettle; they told themselves they would repay the natives for the corn and return the kettle to them when they got the chance. Then they all stuffed as much as they could in their pockets and reburied the rest, then headed for the shore. The Pilgrims would not eat all of this corn but instead keep some of it for seed. Bradford credits this corn with saving the colony, saying, "here they got seed to plant them corn the next year, or else they might have starved, for they had none nor any likelihood to get any till the season had been past." They would, in fact, repay the natives for the corn about six months later, but they grew tired of carrying the heavy kettle and abandoned it on the way back.

THE SECOND EXPLORATORY EXPEDITION

Once the shallop was finally fixed, the men decided to explore the area some more in search of a suitable place to live. Thirty-four men set out in the boat on November 27. "It was a strong and well-armed group," writes Willison, "large enough to strike hard if the Indians were up in arms about the theft of their corn." This time, however, they were led not by Captain Standish but by Captain Jones. Philbrick suggests that this was a negative reflection of Standish's leadership, calling him "recently demoted." In any case, this expedition was not much more successful than the first.

The weather had turned freezing and it snowed all that day and night. The next day was a tiring one of hiking over snow-covered hills and valleys. Jones in particular grew tired and made them stop to set up camp when others wanted to continue exploring. They managed to hunt three geese and six ducks for dinner that night.

The next day they went back to Corn Hill, as they had named the spot where they discovered the sand mound with the corn bushels, and raided the mounds again for more corn. Jones and some others who had fallen ill, most likely from wading through the icy waters to get to shore two days earlier, headed back to the *Mayflower* with the

10 or so bushels of corn. "Standish was once again in charge," Philbrick writes.

The next morning Standish led the party as it followed some Native American tracks into the woods. After about five or six miles (about eight or nine kilometers) they came upon another sand mound they knew to be a grave. Despite the care they took to restore the first grave they had accidentally dug up, with this mound they "resolved to dig it up," according to *Mourt's Relation*, and "brought sundry of the prettiest things away with us" from the two graves it contained. Surprisingly, the first grave contained the remains of a blond-haired man—surely a European—but who he was and how he came to be buried here was a mystery. The other grave held a small child. After having robbed these graves, Standish's party reburied the corpses and moved on.

Before Standish led his men back to the *Mayflower* they had a bit more robbery to commit, this time raiding some wigwams they had come upon that seemed very recently and hastily abandoned. The explorers meant to leave some beads and other things in the Native Americans' homes as a sign of peace for having stolen from them, but in their haste to get back to their ship, they forgot.

Back on the *Mayflower* the settlers debated about whether they should form their colony on Corn Hill. Arguments for Corn Hill included the good ground, the defensible position, and the fact that they were now encountering very cold weather that would make it difficult to do much more exploring. Arguments against the site included the lack of a good, easily accessible freshwater supply and the availability of better harbors in the area. The clinching argument against Corn Hill came from Robert Coppin, their pilot, who had been in the area before and told them of a good harbor with a river on the opposite side of Cape Cod. Coppin's previous party had called it Thievish Harbor after a Native American that had stolen from them, but Captain John Smith had since renamed it Plymouth Harbor. The party decided that they would conduct one more exploratory expedition to assess Plymouth's promise as a potential new home. Little did Captain Standish know, his military leadership was about to get its first real test.

5

New Plymouth

On December 6, 1620, Miles Standish and 15 other men boarded the shallop and made their way across the bay to look for a place to settle around Plymouth, formerly Thievish Harbor. They sailed along the coast for a while looking for a river or creek but found none. Then they did spot something of interest: a group of 10 or 12 Native Americans working on something big and black. They would later find out it was a pilot whale (what they called a "grampus"), and they were carving it into strands.

When the natives saw the settlers, they took off running. The settlers landed a ways off from this spot and built a barricade. They started a fire to fend off the freezing temperature, and set their guard. Four or five miles (six to eight km) off they saw the Native Americans' fire. The night passed without incident.

Arriving in the New World with only secondhand knowledge of the area and its inhabitants, Standish and the Pilgrims were cautious when looking for the ideal location for their colony. The group had already stolen a hidden stash of corn on a hill near the beach and would soon have their first violent encounter with the local Native Americans.

The next day they again looked for a place to build their settlement, some of them in the shallop and some on land, but instead found only grave mounds and abandoned wigwams. That night they built another barricade and fire and took turns standing guard. At about midnight they were woken by a "great and hideous cry," and the guards calling "Arm! Arm!" according to *Mourt's Relation*. A couple of the settlers fired their matchlocks (a type of musket) and the noise stopped. One of the sailors who had heard a similar noise before in Newfoundland said it was a wolf or a fox.

The next morning around breakfast time came another cry, but this time they knew it was not a wolf. Shortly after the cry, a member of the party who had been off by himself came running toward them. "They are men!" he yelled. "Indians! Indians!" Just as he cried out this warning, a swarm of arrows came flying at the settlers. Those that had their muskets nearby quickly grabbed them. Others had just left their muskets and armor down by the shallop and had to run down to get them. The natives pinned them down behind the boat, without matches with which to light the wicks used to ignite the matchlock's priming powder.

Standish got off the first shot from his snaphaunce, a more advanced gun than the matchlock. (Fleming says it "could be fired without the clumsy match and [was] far more accurate" than a matchlock.) Another member of the party fired soon after. Then Standish ordered his men to hold their fire until they could take good aim—only four of them had their guns, and they did not yet know how many enemies they were facing, so they'd have to make every shot count. Their main concern was defending the barricade—if their enemies got their hands on the supplies within the barricade, the settlers would be in even bigger trouble.

It was also important for them to defend the shallop, their only means of escape. One daring member of the settlers' party took a log out of the fire and ran it down to the men taking shelter behind the boat so they could light their matchlocks. All the while the natives were screaming out. "The cry of our enemies was dreadful," says *Mourt's Relation*. To the settlers their shouts sounded like "Woach woach ha ha hach woach."

One particularly big Native American stood behind a tree and shot off at least three arrows at the settlers. The settlers took this man to be their chief. They fired off three shots of their own but missed. Then one of the settlers (Abbott in *Miles Standish, the Puritan*

Capitan says it was Standish, as does Dillon in *The Pilgrims*) took careful aim and splintered the tree behind which he was standing. The native cried out and ran off, his warriors following close behind.

Despite being outnumbered, Standish ordered several men to run after the natives while leaving six behind to guard the shallop. The settlers chased their enemies for a quarter mile (0.4 km), then shouted at them and fired off a couple of shots before turning back. "This we did that they might see we were not afraid of them nor discouraged," according to *Mourt's Relation*. The battle was over. Afterward, the Pilgrims would call it the "First Encounter."

Throughout this first battle, Miles Standish showed the Pilgrims that they had made a good choice in hiring him as their military leader. He remained calm and fearless under fire. He commanded his men strategically and decisively as they held two positions against superior numbers. Upon victory he had the boldness and forethought to send a message to combatants by chasing them into the woods. This last move was perhaps the most important, for it showed the Native Americans that the settlers would not be driven from their new home, wherever they chose to build it.

THE FIRST WINTER AND MILITARY PREPARATIONS

The First Encounter gave the settlers a good indication of how Standish would perform as military leader throughout his career in the colony. He would continue to act boldly in order to always show strength, never weakness. This was particularly important given that the Pilgrims were just a few dozen people surrounded by thousands upon thousands of natives who could wipe them out if they determined to do so.

In searching for a spot to build their settlement, the Pilgrims needed a good place to put their cannon. The cannon would not be very effective in a battle against a group of Native Americans scattered about in the woods, but with its thunderous boom it could still be a good way of showing strength and impressing the natives.

On December 12 they were at last able to explore Plymouth Harbor (though no Pilgrim makes any mention of landing on a rock—it's not clear where the myth of Plymouth Rock comes from). Fortunately they found the place to their liking. They measured depths in the harbor and found it was good for ships. *Mourt's Relation* says, "We marched also into the land, and found divers cornfields, and little running brooks, a place very good for situation, so we returned to our ship again with good news to the rest of our people, which did much comfort their hearts."

Over the next week or so they would continue to explore the area. They found no Native Americans, not even abandoned wigwams. They still could not decide on a place to build their settlement until finally forced to do so by their shrinking supplies, "especially our beer," according to *Mourt's Relation*. They finally picked a site on December 19, but bad weather kept them from all going ashore until a few days later. The situation was getting desperate: The hard trip across the Atlantic and the freezing weather were taking their toll, as some members of their party were starting to die—six had died in December alone. As soon as weather permitted, the Pilgrims scouted out the hill where they wanted to build the platform for the cannon. From the top, they could see all around them, including the bay and far out into the sea. It was the perfect place for the cannon. On December 25, they built the first house frame below the hill.

Over the next week they began building homes and decided to "impale them," or build protective barriers of spiked poles around them. Many historians such as Nathaniel Philbrick believe that Miles Standish was influential in the town's layout. Philbrick writes in *Mayflower*, "At lectures on military engineering at the University of Leiden, soldiers could learn from the Dutch army's chief engineer that the most easily defended settlement pattern consisted of a street with parallel alleys and a cross street. The Pilgrims created a similar design that included two rows of houses 'for safety.'" Standish was given the plot nearest the new Fort Hill.

As they were building their town of New Plymouth (or Plimouth, as they spelled it), they saw smoke from natives' fires a few miles off but had not yet personally encountered any more natives. So on January 4, Captain Standish and four or five other men set out to see if they could meet any of them. They did not, but they did see some abandoned wigwams.

As the winter wore on the Pilgrims continued to build their settlement when weather allowed. More of their people were dying—in addition to the six in December, eight more died in January. One of those eight was Miles Standish's wife, Rose. She died on January 29, 1621, though the exact cause of her death was not recorded.

There would be little time for grieving, however. More and more of the Pilgrims fell sick, to the point that even the ones who were well would have to stop working on the houses in order to take care of the others. In *Of Plymouth Plantation* William Bradford tells of seven people who worked night and day to build fires for their sick comrades, make their beds, wash their clothes, and more. Two of these selfless people were William Brewster and Miles Standish, "unto whom," Bradford writes, "myself and many others were much beholden in our low and sick condition. And yet the Lord so upheld these persons as in this general calamity they were not at all infected wither with sickness or lameness."

At one point during the winter the Pilgrims saw two Native Americans in the distance but could not make contact with them. Then on February 16, one of their party was about a mile and a half (2.4 km) from the plantation hunting birds when he spotted a dozen natives and heard many more nearby. As soon as the natives passed, the Pilgrim made his way back to the settlement as fast as he could and raised the alarm. Standish and another, Francis Cook, were working in the woods and raced back, leaving their tools behind. When they went to retrieve the tools later, they discovered the natives had taken them.

The natives did not attack, but that night the Pilgrims saw their fire in the woods in about the same location where the bird hunter first saw them. They decided that they would need to keep better guard.

Mourt's Relation tells how the next morning "we called a meeting for the establishing of military orders among ourselves, and we chose Miles Standish our captain, and gave him authority of command in affairs." This made official the position Standish had already been filling. (Over the years, Standish would receive a salary of sorts for his service. Mary Caroline Crawford explains in *In the Days of the Pilgrim Fathers*, "Most of the money raised [from taxes] was used for defense. . . . We early find a record that Standish was paid for teaching the use of arms in Plymouth and Duxbury. By degrees the gratuities of certain officials became so regular as to amount to a salary.")

The Pilgrims were unable to get all of their military affairs in order that February morning, though, because the meeting was interrupted by the appearance of two Native Americans on top of a nearby hill. The natives gestured for the Pilgrims to come to them. The Pilgrims gestured, "no, you come to us." The natives refused. The settlers then got their muskets ready, and Captain Standish and Stephen Hopkins went out to meet the natives. One was carrying a musket and placed it on the ground as a sign of peace. When they got close, though, the two natives ran away. Standish and Hopkins heard many more retreating on the other side of the hill.

This encounter caused the Pilgrims to "plant our ordinances in places most convenient," according to *Mourt's Relation*. Captain Jones and some of the sailors brought cannons from the *Mayflower*. They placed a large one that could fire a four-pound (1.8-kilogram) cannonball on top of their hill and another on the shore. They also placed an even larger cannon that could fire a six-pound (2.7-kg)cannonball, and two smaller ones that could fire half-pound (0.2 kg) cannonballs.

The Pilgrims attempted to finish their discussion of military preparations on March 16, but again they were interrupted. This time it was not two natives on top of a hill, but one marching alone right into the middle of their half-built town. If they were surprised by the man's bold behavior, they were even more surprised when he said in perfectly understandable English, "Welcome, Englishmen."

The man's name was Samoset. He was from the Abenaki tribe in Maine and had learned his English from English fishermen. He's described in *Mourt's Relation* as being "a tall straight man, the hair of his head black, long behind, only short before, none on his face at all." He was clothed only in a small piece of leather hanging from a strap around his waist, so the Pilgrims gave him a horseman's coat. He told the Pilgrims that the area they were in was called Patuxet, but most all of the people who lived there died of a great plague about four years earlier. This was actually a relief to the Pilgrims, as it meant that there would likely be no Native Americans claiming that land.

Samoset was in the area visiting Massasoit, the great sachem, or chief, of the Pokanoket tribe and the entire Wampanoag Nation (of which Patuxet was a part). He promised to bring some Wampanoags back to Plymouth within the next couple of days so that the Pilgrims might meet their closest neighbors and trade with them. He also told them of another tribe in the area that was not friendly to Englishmen. This tribe was the Nausets, and a few years earlier an English captain named Thomas Hunt kidnapped seven men from their tribe as well as twenty Patuxet men and sold them into slavery. Samoset told the Pilgrims that it was Nauset tribesmen that they had fought with at the First Encounter, and that had stolen Standish and Cook's tools. The Pilgrims would have to be wary of this tribe.

The Pilgrims spent their first winter in the New World adjusting to the climate, building the first structures to their settlement, and preparing their defenses in the event of an attack. Samoset, a visiting member of the Abenaki tribe in Maine, introduced himself and established communication between the Pilgrims and the local Native American tribe.

They were reminded of this fact a few days later when once again their meeting to discuss military matters was interrupted by the appearance of some natives on top of a nearby hill. Standish led a small party toward the hill. The natives made taunting gestures with their bows and arrows, but when Standish and the others got close, they again ran away.

In the meantime Samoset had brought some Native Americans by to meet and trade with the Pilgrims. These natives also brought back the tools that Standish and Cook had left in the woods. Then on March 22, Samoset returned again with another native named Tisquantum, better known as Squanto. He was a Patuxet, and escaped the deadly plague by virtue of having been one of the 20 of his tribe kidnapped by Hunt. He too could speak English (which he learned in England when he was actually kidnapped once before the Hunt incident, in 1605, by Captain George Weymouth). Squanto led a fascinating life; as Caleb Johnson of MayflowerHistory.com puts it, "he traveled to more countries, visited more colonies, and met more historical figures than any of the Pilgrims ever did."

Squanto and Samoset told the Pilgrims that Massasoit, along with his brother Quadequina and 60 other men, were close by. After a while, the sachem and the rest of the men appeared on top of a nearby hill. The Pilgrims sent Edward Winslow to bring them gifts and talk to them. According to *Mourt's Relation*, Winslow told Massasoit that "King James saluted him with words of love and peace, and did accept him as his friend and ally, and that our governor desired . . . to confirm a peace with him, as his next neighbor." Massasoit agreed to meet with Governor Carver.

The meeting between the two leaders was treated as a ceremony. Captain Standish and some others with muskets went to meet the sachem at the brook and escort him back to the governor's house. Carver entered accompanied by musketeers, and with others playing drums and trumpets. The leaders exchanged kisses, drank some liquor, ate some food, then got down to business. By the time the meeting was over, they had written and signed a short but historic peace treaty. In it, they promised that not only would they not attack each other, but that they would come to each other's aid if attacked by other tribes. This mutual security pact—the first of its kind in America—would stand the test of time, being honored by Massasoit his whole life as well as by his son. For the time being, it bought the Pilgrims some much-needed peace of mind after a long, brutal winter.

Samoset and Squanto, two Native Americans who spoke English, introduced the Pilgrims to Massasoit, the chief of the local tribe and the entire Wampanoag nation. Standish was in attendance when Massasoit and Governor Carter signed a historic peace treaty that would allow the two to live side by side for years to come.

WINTER'S END

After the 14 deaths in December and January, 17 more people died in February and another 13 in March. Of the 102 passengers aboard the *Mayflower* who made it to Cape Cod, only 52 remained at the beginning of summer 1621. With the winter over, however, the settlers grew healthier and their town took shape. They had made peace with their nearest neighbors, and their supposed enemies, the Nausets, were keeping their distance. The chances of survival for New Plymouth were looking up.

NATIVE PEOPLES AROUND PLYMOUTH

When the Pilgrims landed in Plymouth in 1620, the Native Americans were divided into nations consisting of many subtribes. Fortunately for the Pilgrims they landed in Wampanoag territory—had they attempted to settle in the Nauset territory farther to the south and extending throughout the arm of Cape Cod, they might have had a much more hostile reception.

The area to the north, soon to be occupied by Puritan settlers, was the domain of the Massachusetts. Directly to the west of the Wampanoags were their enemies, at least in 1620, the Narragansetts.

Despite sometimes warring with one another, the Native American nations around Plymouth had much in common. They lived in wigwams and spoke some form of the Algonquian language. They fished, farmed, and hunted, and traded with Europeans using shell beads known as wampum for currency.

Just prior to the Pilgrims' arrival, these tribes had seen their populations drop due to disease (mainly smallpox, spotted fever, and measles) after the arrival of Europeans, with the exception of the Narragansetts, who were thus able to become a powerhouse in the region. They and other tribes, however, would suffer greatly in King Philip's War of 1675–1676, which pitted English settlers and their allies from the Pequot and Mohegan tribes against the Narragansetts, Wampanoags, and other tribes led by Massasoit's son Metacom (known to the English as King Philip). This deadly war saw 800 English settlers and 3,000 Native Americans killed. Some tribes would never fully recover from their losses.

Not to say that Miles Standish's job was done. He still had the defense of the colony to think about as well as relations with the natives. The day after Carver and Massasoit signed their treaty, some more Wampanoags showed up at Plymouth. Some of the natives reported that Massasoit wanted the Pilgrims to come visit him. Standish was the man for the job, and he brought with him one Isaac Allerton. Massasoit greeted the two Pilgrims with a few groundnuts and some tobacco. Based on their meeting, the Pilgrims concluded that Massasoit truly did want peace with them (prior to this, there was the possibility that the treaty was an attempt to lure them into a false sense of security). Further proof for the Pilgrims that Massasoit was sincere was the knowledge that the Wampanoags had seen two or three Pilgrims working or hunting alone in the woods, and yet "offered them no harm as they might easily have done," according to *Mourt's Relation*. Also, they knew that Massasoit "hath a potent adversary [in] the Narragansetts, that are at war with him, against whom he thinks we may be some strength to him, for our pieces are terrible unto them."

While Standish played his role in securing peace with the Wampanoags, all was not entirely peaceful in Plymouth. Though the Pilgrims managed to finish a meeting establishing a basic military organization for the colony without interruption, Standish faced dissent within his ranks. The challenge came from John Billington, who Philbrick says "established a reputation as the colony's leading malcontent and rabble-rouser." John Abbott Goodwin calls him a "vulgar brawler." Years later he became Plymouth's first murderer when he shot John Newcomen over a hunting argument. For his crime, he would become the first man hanged in Plymouth. On this occasion in 1621, Billington got in trouble with Standish by disobeying military orders. Standish had none of it. In *A Chronological History of New-England*, Thomas Prince writes that Billington was "convented before the whole company for his contempt of the captain's lawful command with opprobrious speeches, for which he is adjudged to have his neck and heels tied together; but upon humbling himself and craving pardon, and it being the first offence, he is forgiven." Not only was it

Billington's first offense, it was the first serious offense by anyone in the new colony.

Although Billington might have gotten off somewhat easy after begging for forgiveness, the fact that he had his neck and feet tied together was a clear message to the others that Standish's authority was not to be questioned. The Pilgrims might have felt more secure after signing the treaty with Massasoit, but they still knew that enemies lurked nearby, so military discipline under Standish's command was essential to their survival.

6

Bringing Security to Plymouth

With the winter behind them, the Pilgrims did their best to build a normal life in their new home. As their New Year approached on March 25 they held an election in which they again chose John Carver as their governor. Within a month, however, Carver would be dead. After having come in from working in the fields complaining of a headache, he fell into a coma and died within a few days. The settlers held another election, and John Bradford became the new governor of Plymouth.

In the meantime, the *Mayflower* sailed back to England. The Pilgrims were now truly on their own. Under Squanto's supervision they planted corn and caught the herring that started appearing in the Town Brook in mid-April, just as Squanto said they would. The colony even had its first wedding in the spring, with Edward

Winslow, a widower of just six weeks, marrying Susanna White, who had lost her husband that winter.

With things going well for the settlers, it was up to the Billington clan to make things uncomfortable again. Within a couple of days of Winslow and Hopkins returning from Sowams, John Billington's 16-year-old son John Jr. strolled off into the woods and got lost. He wandered for five days, living on berries, until he was able to follow a trail to the small Native American village of Manomet. The Manomet sachem, Canacum, handed young Billington over to the Nausets, the same tribe that attacked the Pilgrims at the First Encounter and from whom the Pilgrims stole the corn at Corn Hill. John Abbot Goodwin writes in *The Pilgrim Republic*, "A party of ten, well armed, at once went in the shallop to recover him, Standish probably being the leader, with Winslow as an associate."

At the village of Nauset, Squanto went to tell the sachem Aspinet why the Pilgrims had come. Soon there were Nausets everywhere—a great surprise to the Pilgrims, as they had explored this land back in December and found nothing resembling a village at that time. They distrusted the Nausets and kept their muskets ready as they told the natives that only two could approach the boat. One of these two was the man whose corn they had stolen. They promised they would either bring him corn in repayment or he could come to Plymouth to get repaid. He said he would come visit them.

After sunset Aspinet showed up with more than 100 men as well as John Billington Jr. The boy had beads hung all around his neck and seemed to have been treated very well. Aspinet "made peace with us, we bestowing a knife on him, and likewise on another that first entertained the boy and brought him thither," according to *Mourt's Relation*. As it turned out, a Billington actually brought Plymouth an extra measure of peace and respect.

The good feelings would not last long, however. While still in Nauset the Pilgrims learned that the Narragansett tribe had kidnapped Massasoit. The Pilgrims feared that this could mean the Narragansetts were preparing to attack Plymouth, which would have been disastrous given that more than half the colony's men were there in Nauset. They rushed home and discovered that although the Narragansetts did take Massasoit, there was yet another problem. A sachem named Corbitant from the Wampanoag village of Mattapoisett was making a power play against Massasoit, complaining of the peace he and Aspinet had made with the Pilgrims. Corbitant also spoke out against Squanto and a Wampanoag warrior named Hobbamock that *Mourt's Relation* calls "a special and trusty man of Massasoit's."

Squanto and Hobbamock went to see if they could find out what happened to Massasoit. Corbitant found out that these two men were in the village of Nemasket and had his warriors raid the wigwam where they were staying. One warrior had a knife to Squanto's chest. Corbitant said, according to *Mourt's Relation*, that if Squanto were dead, "the English had lost their tongue." This would have been a death blow for Plymouth. As Willison explains in *Saints and Strangers*, "Without Squanto and his native skills and knowledge of the country, the Pilgrims would almost certainly have perished or been forced to flee the plantation, for they would have had no crops."

At this point Hobbamock was able to break away and make a run for it. He was a pniese, which Caffrey describes in *Mayflower* as being the "bravest and strongest in the tribe with an arduous and lengthy training in his youth. . . . He could, they said, not be wounded in battle." (She goes on to say, "In time, Hobbamock became Standish's man as Squanto was Bradford's.") Hobbamock ran all the way back to Plymouth and told them that Squanto was in all likelihood dead.

Now was the time for Captain Standish to truly put his military background to use. He was to lead a party of 10 armed men (according to *Mourt's Relation*; in *Of Plymouth Plantation* Bradford puts the number at 14), plus Hobbamock as their guide, to Nemasket. This was not to be a diplomatic expedition, however; if Corbitant had in fact killed Squanto, this was to be a mission of revenge. Bradford explains the necessity of this in *Of Plymouth Plantation*, saying "if they should suffer their friends and messengers to be thus wronged," they would not be able to get anyone else to ally with them or help them in any way, and the Pilgrims themselves would then be the next to be attacked.

Standish and his men set off the next day. They stopped a few miles from Nemasket and hid until dark. Standish gave the men their orders, and they gave each other encouragement—for most of them, it would be their first military operation. They ate the food they brought with them, then around midnight they moved in.

Hobbamock showed them the wigwam where Corbitant was staying, and the Pilgrims stormed in. They ordered everyone to stay still and demanded to know if Corbitant was among them. The natives were too terrified to speak. Some of them escaped through another door but were wounded by the Pilgrims on their way out. The Pilgrims fired off a couple of muskets, further frightening the Nemasket villagers. The Pilgrims were finally able to calm the natives down somewhat, at which point they found out that Corbitant and his men had already left the village, and that Squanto was alive. Hobbamock climbed atop the wigwam and called out for Squanto, who soon appeared along with some others.

Standish had the natives turn in their bows and arrows, promising to give them back in the morning. The Pilgrims took over the wigwam for the night, releasing the natives they were holding there. In the morning, the Pilgrims told the natives ("undoubtedly spoken by Standish in his grimmest manner," says Willison in *Saints and Strangers*) that "although Corbitant had now escaped us, yet there was no place should secure him and his from us if he continued threatening us and provoking others against us, who had kindly entertained him, and never intended evil towards him till he now so justly deserved it," according to *Mourt's Relation*. They also vowed to take revenge against anyone or any tribe that harmed Massasoit, Squanto, Hobbamock, or any of Massasoit's people.

For those they had wounded, even though (in the Pilgrims' opinion) they brought their wounds upon themselves by "not staying in the house at our command," the Pilgrims offered to take them back to Plymouth to be looked after by their surgeon. One man and one woman took them up on this, and the party made its way back to the colony.

While they did not capture Corbitant, the midnight raid had the desired effect of showing that the Pilgrims would not put up with any attacks on themselves or their allies. As Bradford writes in *Of Plymouth Plantation*, "After this they had many gratulations from divers sachems; . . . Corbitant himself used the mediation of Massasoit to make his peace, but was shy to come near them a long while after." All of the tribes of the Cape Cod area came by and declared themselves loyal subjects of King James, according to Willison. Standish's assault had bought them a "much firmer peace," as Bradford puts it. But would it last?

NEW THREATS

In the fall of 1621, the Pilgrims were in their most comfortable position yet since coming to the New World. They were relatively healthy, their town was taking shape, they had a newfound peace with their neighbors, and their food supply was in better shape following a successful harvest of corn and barley—though their pea crop did not do as well. All in all, it was the perfect time to hold a traditional English harvest festival, "a secular celebration," Philbrick writes, "that dated back to the Middle ages." They invited their good friend Massasoit, without whose help the Pilgrims would not have survived their first year. This was the great feast that would eventually become known as the First Thanksgiving and give birth to a national holiday.

In 1621, the Pilgrims held the First Thanksgiving to celebrate their health, the harvest, and their friendship with the Wampanoag nation. During this three-day feast, the Pilgrims and a group of Wampanoag Indians shared venison, geese, duck, beans, and acorns and gave birth to a future national holiday.

Although the Pilgrims were grateful for their close ties with Massasoit's Wampanoags, the alliance would bring them trouble as well. Canonicus, the Narragansett sachem, grew jealous of the relationship. That winter he sent a messenger to the Pilgrims with a bundle of arrows tied together with snakeskin. The Pilgrims did not know what to make of this, and Squanto was not there at the time to interpret for them, so they "committed [the messenger] to the custody of Captain Standish," according to Edward Winslow in *Good Newes from New-England*, until they could figure out what the bundle meant. Standish ordered the frightened messenger to be treated kindly. Standish then consulted with Bradford and his assistant Isaac Allerton, and they decided that since it was against both Native American and European law to harm a messenger, they should release the native.

When Squanto returned he told the Pilgrims that the bundle amounted to a challenge by Canonicus. Bradford's response was to wrap some gunpowder and gunshot in the snakeskin and send it back to the sachem. Winslow says, "it was no small terror to this savage king; insomuch as he would not once touch the powder and shot, or suffer it to stay in his house or country." The bundle traveled to several other villages, but nobody would receive it, and it "at length came whole back again" to Plymouth.

The return challenge seemed to work, but the Pilgrims decided that it would still be a good idea to improve their defenses. "Doubtless at Standish's urging," says Philbrick, they decided to impale the entire town. This meant building an eight- or perhaps even eleven-foot-high (3.3-meter-high) barrier nearly a mile around, enclosing the town as well as Fort Hill. They had a bit more manpower now to get the job done—the English ship the *Fortune* had unexpectedly arrived in November, sent by the Merchant Adventurers and bearing 35 new settlers for the colony.

The Pilgrims finished the wall in February 1622. It had three gates called flankers that would be kept locked and guarded at night. Standish then got to work reorganizing the colony's military. He divided it into four companies and appointed a commander and a meeting spot for each one. He then divided the Plymouth men up among the companies and told them that in the case of an emergency, they were to report to their commanders at their meeting spot, and the commanders would lead them if Standish was not around.

The Captain trained the men vigorously and taught the newcomers to use their muskets. He also devised a plan in case their enemies tried to distract or preoccupy them by setting part of the village on fire. Although most of the settlers would work to put out the fire, Standish

THE FIRST THANKSGIVING

The description of the First Thanksgiving comes from a letter by Edward Winslow published in *Mourt's Relation*. In it Winslow tells how Bradford sent four men bird hunting (turkeys are not specifically mentioned) "so that we might after a special manner rejoice together after we had gathered the fruits of our labors." They invited Massasoit—who then showed up with 90 braves! If the Pilgrims were worried about feeding all these men, their fears were soon put to rest as the natives went out and killed five deer for the feast, which lasted three days.

The Web site PilgrimHall.org explains how today's modern Thanksgiving holiday is actually a combination of that first feast in 1621, the traditional Puritan religious Day of Thanksgiving in which "the entire day would have been spent in church, with no feasting or amusements," and the traditional nonreligious day of giving thanks "to celebrate a specific event, such as victory in battle or the end of a war." George Washington issued a Thanksgiving Day proclamation to the people of the new United States in 1789 in which he gave thanks to "that great and glorious Being, who is the beneficent Author of all the good that was, that is, or that will be" for, among other things, their victory in the Revolutionary War. In 1683, in the middle of the Civil War, Abraham Lincoln became the first president to declare an annual national Day of Thanksgiving, and the modern national holiday was born.

appointed one company to stand guard around the fire with their backs to it to "prevent treachery, if any were in that kind intended," says Winslow. If it happened to be the house of one of the members of this special fire unit company that was up in flames, that man would be relieved from guard duty and freed to help put out the fire.

The new defenses and military training could not prepare the Pilgrims for the next threat they would encounter, however. Just as Standish was getting ready to travel to the Massachusetts to trade for furs, Hobbamock told them that the Massachusetts and Narragansetts had teamed up and were plotting to kill Standish and then attack Plymouth. Even worse, Hobbamock said that Squanto was part of the conspiracy. The Pilgrims thought that Hobbamock might have made this last bit up due to the jealous rivalry between him and Squanto. They decided that Standish and several other men, including Hobbamock and Squanto, would proceed with the expedition. But just as the shallop was taking off, one of Squanto's relatives came running out of the woods into Plymouth, out of breath and blood running down his face, saying that the Narragansetts, with Corbitant, had teamed up with Massasoit and were coming to attack the colony.

The Pilgrims fired a signal shot that fortunately was heard by the men in the shallop. Standish ordered the boat to return to Plymouth as quickly as possible. When they got back and found out what was going on, Hobbamock insisted that Massasoit would not break his treaty with the Pilgrims. The Pilgrims for their part thought this was suspicious as well. Hobbamock's wife went to the Pokanoket village and found that Massasoit was in fact still there and had no plans to attack Plymouth.

As the days passed and the Pilgrims pieced together what happened, "it became increasingly clear that Squanto had been laboring long and hard to overthrow Massasoit as the Pokanokets' supreme sachem," Philbrick writes. They also found out that Squanto had been telling the other natives that the Pilgrims kept the plague buried under their common house and that Squanto could have them unleash it on anyone whenever he wanted.

When he found out about Squanto's treachery, Massasoit was furious. He demanded that the Pilgrims hand Squanto over so he could be killed. Governor Bradford was fond of his interpreter, however, and protected him. The Pilgrims also found it to their advantage to play Squanto and Hobbamock off against one another. As Bradford writes in *Of Plymouth Plantation*, he was close to Squanto, and Standish was close to Hobbamock, "by which they had better intelligence, and made them both more diligent."

As it turned out, Squanto's days of helping the Pilgrims were numbered anyway. In November 1622, he became sick with what Bradford calls "an Indian fever, bleeding much at the nose (which the Indians take for a symptom of death)." He died just a few days later, and the Pilgrims were left without their interpreter.

STANDISH LOSES HIS TEMPER

Meanwhile, Plymouth was again suffering another tough winter. They still had not learned how to grow corn very well, and their food supplies were low. Fortunately a ship, the *Discovery*, had arrived from England in the fall, and the settlers were able to trade with them for items such as beads, knives, and trinkets that they could then use to trade with the natives.

Bradford went to several villages and traded for corn and beans (a trip that Standish was supposed to have made himself, but he was sick with a fever), but the shallop was damaged in a storm so Bradford had to leave the food behind and walk home. In January 1623, Standish then set out with some other settlers on a trip to pick up some of this food—a trip that would bring out his famous temper.

Their destination was Nauset. The sachem Aspinet delivered the corn to Standish, but when the Captain returned to the shallop, he discovered that they had been robbed of some beads and other small items. Standish was furious. He led an armed party back to the village and told Aspinet that if the stolen items weren't returned right away, the Pilgrims would attack. He then departed for the night, refusing Aspinet's offers of hospitality.

The next morning the sachem and many villagers went to meet Standish and the others. Aspinet saluted Standish and greeted him by licking his hand "from the wrist to the finger's end," according to Winslow. He then returned the stolen items to Standish and assured him that the thief had been "much beaten" as punishment.

In February Standish went to Cummaquid, home of the sachem Iyanough, to retrieve more food. Again Standish noticed some trinkets had been stolen, and again his temper flared. Here, too, Standish threatened an attack if the items weren't returned immediately. Iyanough suggested that they look in the shallop again. The trinkets were in fact there. Although the natives were apparently not at fault, they still brought out more corn to trade with Standish in order to "appease his anger," as Winslow says.

The Captain's anger would soon be provoked again on yet another trip to retrieve corn, this one in March. In the village of Manomet, Standish and a couple of other Pilgrims were meeting with the sachem Canacum when two Massachusetts warriors came into the wigwam. Standish was already disappointed in the sachem's behavior, which was apparently less friendly toward Standish than it had been toward Bradford earlier. Willison in *Saints and Strangers* suggests that this might have been because Canacum had by this time heard of Standish's tantrums at Nauset and Cummaquid. Whatever the case, Canacum's attention was now directed to the Massachusett newcomers, in particular one named Wituwamat whom Winslow calls "a notable insulting villain, one who had formerly imbued his hands in the blood of English and French . . . and derided their weakness, especially because, as he said, they died crying, making sour faces, more like children than men."

Wituwamat presented Canacum with a knife and made a long speech. The Pilgrims had no interpreter with them and Standish, "though he be the best linguist amongst us," according to Winslow, could not tell what Wituwamat was saying. What he did know,

When the cold New England winter set in, the Pilgrims realized that their successful harvest would not be able to sustain them through to spring. Forced to ration whatever was left, many went hungry as daily allowances dwindled to five kernels of corn per day. Above, a master of the house distributes the five kernels to each person.

however, was that Canacum was now showing much more hospitality toward the Massachusetts than toward the Pilgrims. The insult caused Standish's temper to flare. He scolded Canacum for his poor behavior and demanded that the corn be delivered immediately so they could leave.

Without explaining how, Winslow says that they later found out what Wituwamat said to Canacum in the wigwam. Apparently he was recruiting Canacum for an attack on the relatively new colony at Wessagussett, started by some Englishmen just 22 miles (35.4 km) from Plymouth. After that, they would wipe out Plymouth itself.

Before the Pilgrims left, a warrior of the Pamet tribe came into the wigwam. Even though he had been friendly toward the Pilgrims and Standish in particular, he was now part of the Massachusetts plot, according to Winslow. The Pamet warrior said he would accompany the Pilgrims and help them bring back the corn; his real intention, Winslow says, was to kill Standish, after which other natives would kill the other Pilgrims. Standish stayed up all that cold night, pacing back and forth in front of the fire, thus allegedly ruining the Massachusetts's plan and saving his own life.

ASSAULT AT WESSAGUSSETT

What happened next is one of the darkest chapters in the history of Plymouth. In March 1623, after a consultation involving Bradford, Allerton and Standish, the Pilgrims decided that "Captain Standish should take so many men, as he thought sufficient to make his party good against all the Indians in the Massachuset bay," according to Winslow. There was one man in particular they wanted dead: Standish was ordered to make sure that Wituwamat was there when he launched the attack, and then bring back his head "that he might be a warning and terror to all of that disposition."

The reason the Pilgrims later gave for this plan was an event that occurred just a few days before. On the way home from a trip to Sowams to see Massasoit when the great sachem was very ill and believed to be dying (Winslow ended up healing Massasoit completely), Hobbamock supposedly told Winslow of a plot against Plymouth. According to Winslow, Hobbamock said Massasoit took him aside and told him that the Massachusetts had convinced several other tribes to join an attack first against Wessagussett and then against Plymouth.

In *Saints and Strangers*, Willison finds several flaws in Winslow's story. Why, for instance, wouldn't Massasoit just tell Winslow of the plot himself? Or, given that many of the tribes mentioned in the plot were part of the Wampanoag nation, why did the sachem "not offer to call them to heel, for they were his subjects and looked to him in all things? The inclusion of them in the Pilgrims' story undoubtedly was an afterthought, inserted to explain away several embarrassing events on the Cape." If those tribes were actually part of the Massachusetts's plot, "then they were in revolt against Massasoit . . . But there is not a shred of evidence anywhere to suggest that this was true."

In any case, after it was decided that Standish would proceed to the colony at Wessagussett, he picked eight men including Hobbamock and set out. They met with the English settlers at the plantation and told them of their attack plan. These settlers were in terrible shape—they had almost no food and were being humiliated and treated harshly by some of the local natives. They agreed not to interfere with Standish's plan.

The Pilgrims were counting on the element of surprise, especially if they were to be sure Wituwamat would be there, so they pretended to be on a trading mission. One native traded some furs to the Pilgrims, but Winslow said his real purpose was to find out why the Pilgrims were really there. "And though the Captain carried things as smoothly as possibly he could," Winslow writes, "yet at [the native's] return he reported he saw by [Standish's] eyes that he was angry in his heart." Later a Massachusett pniese named Pecksuot came among them and told Hobbamock that he knew that Standish was there to kill them. Pecksuot told Hobbamock to tell Standish, "let him begin when he dare, he shall not take us at unawares."

Thereafter Pecksuot and other natives would come up to Standish and "sharpen the points of their knives before his face," according to Winslow. Wituwamat had arrived and bragged about his knife with a picture of a woman's face on it. He said he had another with a man's face with which he had killed English and French, and "these two must marry." Pecksuot added his own insults, saying that although Standish "were a great captain, he was but a little man; and, said he, though I be no sachem, yet I am a man of great strength and courage." Standish listened to these insults but remained patient until the time was right.

The next day, realizing that he would not be able to get many of the Massachusetts together at one time, Standish decided to call just Pecksuot, Wituwamat, one other brave, and Wituwamat's younger brother ("some eighteen years of age," says Winslow) into a house for a meal with some of the Pilgrims. At Standish's signal, one of his men shut the door. Standish lunged for the knife hanging from a string around Pecksuot's neck. He grabbed it and began stabbing the pniese with it furiously. The other Pilgrims attacked Wituwamat and the other brave. Wituwamat and Pecksuot in particular put up a great struggle. "It is incredible how many wounds these two pnieses received before they died," Winslow says. With the three braves dead, Hobbamock, who had simply stood and watched the attack, reminded Standish that Pecksuot had called him a "little man" the day before. "Today," he said, "I see you are big enough to lay him on the ground."

The Pilgrims took Wituwamat's brother hostage—later Standish would have him hanged. Standish then sent word to the other

When it was allegedly discovered that Massachusetts Bay Indians were conspiring to raid and murder everyone in the Wessagussett and Plymouth colonies, Standish was ordered to organize a military campaign against the group. Standish and several others killed Wituwamat, the leader of the plot, and carried his head on a stick back to Plymouth.

Pilgrims to kill all native men in the settlement. They killed two more, and Standish and the men with him killed another. One native escaped, however, and warned the others, bringing the killing spree to an end. Now Standish and half his company, plus a couple of the Wessagussett settlers, went looking for others. They met a few near a hill and raced for the strategic ground at the top. Standish got there first, causing the natives to retreat and seek shelter behind trees. The natives hurled insults and shot arrows, taking aim at Standish and Hobbamock. Finally Hobbamock took off his coat, and chased them into the woods "so fast, as our people were not able to hold way with him." One native, however, took aim with his bow at Standish, who then shot back at him and broke his arm, causing the natives to flee into the swamp. There, they ignored the Captain's calls for their leader to come out and fight like a man. Eventually the Pilgrims returned to the plantation, released the women they had taken prisoner, and "would not take their beaver coats from them, nor suffer the least discourtesy to be offered them," Winslow writes.

With Wessagussett now too dangerous for its colonists to remain, the Pilgrims offered to take them back to Plymouth. The Wessagussett settlers instead decided to sail their ship up to Maine and try their luck there. Standish and the rest of his company made their way back to Plymouth, where they placed Wituwamat's head on a pike on the roof of their new fort.

Word spread quickly of the attack at Wessagussett. Philbrick writes in *Mayflower*, "All throughout Cape Cod . . . the Native inhabitants had fled in panic, convinced that Standish and his thugs were about to descend on their villages and kill every Indian in sight." The result was that "Indians throughout the region were unable to plant crops. . . . By summer, they had begun to die at a startling rate. . . . Just about every notable sachem on the cape died in the months ahead, including Canacum at Manomet, Aspinet at Nauset, and Iyanough at Cummaquid."

While the massacre at Wessagussett brought Plymouth even more security and more power for their ally Massasoit, there was one man who was not entirely happy with Standish's behavior. John Robinson, the Pilgrims' pastor who had remained in Leiden, wrote to William Bradford, "Oh, how happy a thing had it been, if you had converted some before you had killed any!" He said while he loved Standish, "there may be wanting that tenderness of the life of a man (made after God's image) which is meet. . . . I am afraid lest, by these occasions, others should be drawn to affect a kind of ruffling course in the world." In other words, Robinson was afraid that Standish's attack would lead to more violence against the natives by other Europeans. While Standish's actions—not only at Wessagussett but throughout Plymouth's short history—may have saved the colony, they also took a devastating toll on their native neighbors and set a bloody example for relations between European settlers and Native Americans for the generations to come.

His Later Career

Though the massacre at Wessagussett might have set an example of violence and bloodshed and contributed to Miles Standish's reputation for hotheadedness, he would commit no further violence against Native Americans for the duration of his long life. He would, however, still perform important duties for the colony, both as captain of Plymouth's army and in new roles.

But first, Standish had a more personal matter to attend to. The ship the *Anne* arrived in Plymouth in the summer of 1623 with 60 passengers aboard. Among them was a woman named Barbara who, within a matter of perhaps days, would become Mrs. Miles Standish. Nothing else is known about her before her arrival in Plymouth, not even her maiden name. She would, however, stay married to Miles the rest of his life, and together they would have seven children (though two would die at an early age).

Married life would not completely settle the captain down. In 1625, his famous temper flared up again over a dispute concerning a fishing platform on Cape Anne. In *A General History of New England*, William Hubbard writes, "The dispute grew to be very hot, and high words passed between [Standish and the other party], which might have ended in blows, if not in blood and slaughter, had not the prudence and moderation of Mr. Roger Conant . . . timely prevented." He then goes on to deliver his famous judgment of Captain Standish: "A little chimney is soon fired; so was the Plymouth Captain, a man of very little stature, yet of a very hot and angry temper. The fire of his passion soon kindled and blown up into a flame by hot words, might easily have consumed all, had it not been seasonably quenched."

Despite his hot temper at Cape Anne, or perhaps because of it—perhaps Governor Bradford and the other Plymouth leaders decided it was time the Captain had a change of scenery—Standish was chosen to take a trip to England to meet with the Merchant Adventurers. His task was to try to get them to send better supplies to Plymouth, and at better prices for the settlers. This was a new role for Standish, that of diplomat and financial negotiator. As Kate Caffrey writes in *The Mayflower*, Standish "had been warned to keep his temper, placate the Adventurers, [and] ask for help in dealing with difficult people on both sides of the Atlantic."

The trip almost ended in disaster for Standish before he even reached England. Two ships were sailing back to England at that time, the larger *Charity* towing the smaller *Little James*. George F. Willison in *Saints and Strangers* writes that Standish "decided at the last moment not to keep watch over the furs on the *Little James*, as arranged, but to go in greater comfort on the *Charity*." It turned out to be an important decision, because once strong winds forced the

Charity to cut the *Little James* loose in the English Channel, pirates captured the smaller ship. Everyone on board the *Little James* was sold into slavery. "Nothing more was heard of the *Little James*, her passengers or cargo," Willison writes.

Standish thus narrowly avoided being sold into slavery by pirates and landed safely in England, but things did not go much better after that. London was in the middle of a plague, "so as no business could be done," according to Bradford in *Of Plymouth Plantation*. The Merchant Adventurers were also in a terrible financial spot with the loss of the *Little James* and all their goods that were aboard.

On top of all of this, Bradford did not have much confidence in Standish's negotiating skills, and in a letter to Robert Cushman, their Separatist friend who had stayed behind in England, Bradford asked Cushman to help Standish with obtaining supplies, "for therein he hath least skill." As Standish would learn upon reaching England, however, Cushman was among those who died in the plague. Standish did the best he could without Cushman's help, given the situation with the plague, which it turns out was not very good. He managed to borrow only the relatively small amount of £150 at the outrageous rate of 50 percent interest, and he had to spend a large amount of the borrowed money on his expenses.

Worse than this for the Pilgrims, however, was the news that Captain Standish brought back with him to Plymouth in April 1626: Not only was Cushman dead, but so was King James I—bad news given that the new King Charles I was rumored to be leaning more toward Catholicism and thus would not be as sympathetic toward the Pilgrims. Worst of all, however, was Standish's news that the Pilgrims' pastor John Robinson had died on March 1. The plan had been for their spiritual leader to join his congregation in Plymouth at some point. It was a heavy blow to the Pilgrims, but as always they would have to make do with what they had and continue on.

SHOWDOWN AT MERRYMOUNT

Despite the loss of their spiritual leader, things calmed down for the Pilgrims after Robinson's death. Later in 1626, they came to an agreement to buy out the Merchant Adventurers—Standish and his Pilgrim comrades now owned the colony themselves. In 1627, Standish, William Bradford and Isaac Allerton were given control over the colony's trade and received payments from the other shareholders in Plymouth. In return, Standish and the others were to pay off all of the colony's debts.

Standish's new role as businessman did not put an end to his military service. The following year he was once again called into action. A few years earlier, a small group of men started a new colony near Plymouth. By 1628 a man named Thomas Morton had become head of the plantation he called Mar-e Mount, and which the Pilgrims called Merrymount. The colony was infamous for long, loud, drunken parties, an offense to the quiet and religious Pilgrims at Plymouth. In addition, Morton and the others at Merrymount had been selling muskets, powder, and shot to the natives, which the Pilgrims considered unforgivable. Bradford gives one more reason for the Pilgrims despising Merrymount, saying that they would be unable to keep their servants, "for Morton would entertain any, how vile soever, and all the scum of the country or any discontents would flock to him from all places, if this nest was not broken." In other words, Bradford figured the Pilgrims' servants were unhappy in their positions and would be tempted to run away to Morton's drunken paradise. The Pilgrims decided to take action.

There are two accounts of the Battle of Merrymount, one by Bradford in *Of Plymouth Plantation* and the other by Morton himself in his book *New Canaan*. In Bradford's telling, Captain Standish and his troops went to Merrymount where they found Morton and the others ready for a fight, with their doors blocked and powder and bullets at the ready. The only thing that kept a firefight from breaking

Members of Plymouth colony were dismayed to find that the colonists of Merrymount, a nearby plantation, engaged in activities that were not only against Separatist beliefs, but also potentially dangerous to the safety of all colonists. Although there are two very different versions of the way he handled the situation, Standish managed to put an end to the drunken parties and the trading of weapons with the Native Americans at Merrymount.

out was the fact that Morton and his men were too drunk to even lift their weapons. Morton attempted to shoot Standish, but the captain simply walked up to him and took his weapon away. He then took Morton back to Plymouth "where he was kept till a ship went from the Isle of Shoals for England."

Morton's version of the encounter is quite a bit different. According to him, Standish and his men waited until most of the men of Merrymount were off trading and hunting before setting out to attack the settlement. Along the way they happened upon Morton at Wessagusset and captured him there. The Pilgrims got drunk, however, and Morton escaped. "Their grande leader, Captain Shrimpe," Morton writes, using the nickname he made up for Standish, "took on most furiously and tore his clothes in anger, to see the empty nest, and their bird gone."

Standish then led his party in pursuit of Morton to Merrymount in order to "vindicate his reputation, who had sustained blemish" by letting Morton escape. They ordered Morton to surrender, which he nobly agreed to do only after seeing how much of the Pilgrims' blood he would have spilled by firing on them from his house. He got the Pilgrims to agree not to harm him or any of his property or men, but as soon as he turned himself over, Captain Shrimp and his men threw him to the ground and beat him. After taking him back to Plymouth, they then abandoned him on the Isle of Shoals "without gun, powder or shot or dog or so much as a knife to get anything to feed upon or any other clothes to shelter him with, at winter, than a thin suit."

As Willison says of these two very different versions in *Saints and Strangers*, "one is as fantastic as the other." The truth most likely lies somewhere inbetween.

FOUNDING DUXBURY

Things quieted down in Plymouth quite a bit after that. Later in 1628, the Plymouth court began to distribute 20-acre (8 hectares) plots of land to the settlers so that they might grow more crops and raise livestock. With the threat of attacks by Native Americans greatly reduced and the demand for corn, goat milk, cattle, and other farm products on the rise, the Pilgrims found that not only were they no longer fighting for survival, they were actually growing relatively rich.

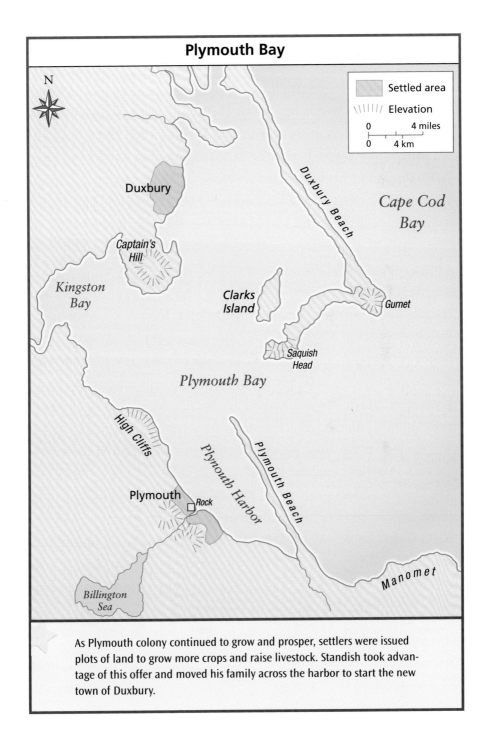

Plymouth Bay

N

Settled area

Elevation

0   4 miles

0   4 km

Duxbury

Captain's Hill

Duxbury Beach

Cape Cod Bay

Kingston Bay

Clarks Island

Gurnet

Saquish Head

Plymouth Bay

High Cliffs

Plymouth Harbor

Plymouth Beach

Plymouth

Rock

Manomet

Billington Sea

As Plymouth colony continued to grow and prosper, settlers were issued plots of land to grow more crops and raise livestock. Standish took advantage of this offer and moved his family across the harbor to start the new town of Duxbury.

Willison writes in *Saints and Strangers*, "Anxious to develop their new farms and profit from soaring prices, people began moving out of Plymouth at an alarming rate."

Among those moving out of Plymouth were Miles Standish, his wife, Barbara, and their children. In 1932 they and some others moved across the harbor from Plymouth and started the town of Duxbury. For his farm Standish chose a plot of land at the foot of what would come to be called Captain's Hill. His friend Hobbamock moved there as well and stayed with the Standish family until his death in 1642. It is believed that he was buried on Captain's Hill, near a big rock that came to be known as the Captain's Chair.

As for the town name "Duxbury," it later fueled speculation that Standish was born in Duxbury in England. John S. C. Abbott, for instance, writes in *Miles Standish*, "The town was named Duxbury, in honor of the captain, as that was the name of the seat which his family occupied in England." However, according to Willison, "for half a century the town was not known as Duxbury at all, but as Duxburrow (often written as 'Ducksburrow'), which would suggest that it was named for the large flocks of waterfowl that nested in the extensive salt marches along its shores."

Despite moving across the harbor, Standish remained active in Plymouth. In 1633 he was chosen to be assistant governor of Plymouth, a title he would hold for several more years. He and others made the journey back to Plymouth every Sunday for the Sabbath meeting for several years, until they were granted permission to officially incorporate Duxbury as its own town in 1637. Even after that, he was chosen as colony treasure for Plymouth in 1644, a role he served until 1649.

CAPTAIN TO THE END

Nor was he done serving as Captain. In 1632 the Narragansetts marched against Massasoit, who fled to the Pilgrims' trading post at

THE END OF PLYMOUTH COLONY

Plymouth survived as a separate colony for a number of decades after the death of its founding fathers. In 1686 it was made part of the Dominion of New England, an unpopular attempt by King James II to have centralized rule over all the New England colonies. After King William came to power in 1689, he dissolved the Dominion of New England, and some of the colonies started applying to England for a charter—that is, official status. England was at war against France at this time, a war that spilled over into New England and included Native American allies on both sides.

Thomas Hinckley, the governor of Plymouth Colony, for some reason did not press very hard for his colony to be granted a charter. In 1690 he wrote a letter saying that they were unwilling to raise the funds for the fees, etc., necessary for obtaining a charter unless they could be very certain they would get it.

In *Pilgrim Colony* George D. Langdon, Jr., explains that Plymouth also had no important contact in England who "was prepared to argue its case. More important, the recurring reports of military failure in the war against the French indicated that consolidation was in the best interests of the crown and also of the inhabitants of New England." On October 7, 1691, King William granted a charter to Massachusetts that made Plymouth part of that colony. The Plymouth Colony was no more.

Sowams. John S. C. Abbott writes, "It seems to have been the impression, with both colonists and Indians, that Captain Standish, in himself alone, was a resistless force. He was immediately dispatched, *with three men*, to repel an army of nobody knew how many hundreds of warriors." When he got to Sowams, Standish saw that the threat was real and sent a messenger back to Plymouth for reinforcements. The situation soon took care of itself, however, when the Narragansetts learned that the Pequots were moving in on their territory and so gave up their attack on Massasoit to defend their own land.

The Narragansetts fought alongside the Pilgrims as well as settlers from the other New England colonies against the Pequots in the Pequot War of 1637—an assault in retaliation for the Pequots killing the captains of several English trading ships. Captain Standish commanded 50 men from Plymouth in that war, which in part led to the formation of the United Colonies of New England—Massachusetts Bay, Plymouth, Connecticut, and New Haven—in 1643.

Standish was called upon to once again stand up to the Narragansetts in 1645. The tribe made war against the Mohegans, with whom the English had a treaty and were thus obligated to defend. The English tried diplomacy with the Narragansetts at first but their efforts failed, bringing them closer to war. Though about 60 years old, Standish was put in charge of 40 men from Plymouth to set out and confront the natives. The other United Colonies supplied many men, but it was Standish and his men who made it to the rendezvous point first. Some friendly natives joined the colonists, and were placed under Standish's command.

Once again, the war did not materialize. The English made one more attempt at diplomacy. Seeing the large force the English had quickly assembled, the Narragansetts this time listened to reason, and a treaty was signed before any shots were fired.

The next threat came not from any native tribe, but from the Dutch. Word reached the colonies in 1653 that war had broken out between England and Holland. The United Colonies prepared for a Dutch attack. Plymouth colony supplied 60 men for the militia, including six from Duxbury. Captain Standish was about 70 years old at this point, but he was still considered the best man for the job, and was put in charge of the Plymouth force. "Instructions were given to Standish, dated June 20th, 1654, ordering him to be ready at Plymouth on the 28th of June," according to Justin Winsor in *History of the Town of Duxbury, Massachusetts.* Winsor continues, "he still enjoyed the highest confidence of the people, and in the instructions last named, in speaking of him, they say, 'of whose approved fidelitie and abillitie wee have had long experience.'" As it turns out, Standish did not need to prove his abilities again, as the Dutch did not attack the colonies.

This was the final call to battle for Miles Standish. He died on October 3, 1656 "after his suffering of much dolorous paine," according to Nathaniel Morton in *New England's Memorial.* John Abbot Goodwin writes in *The Pilgrim Republic* that since Plymouth's only doctor had left a few years earlier, "Standish could not readily obtain even the rude treatment of the times, and from his anguish death is said to have been a welcome relief."

He was buried in Duxbury near his daughter Lora and his daughter-in-law Mary. He was survived by his wife, Barbara, and four sons, Alexander, Myles, Josiah, and Charles. He left most everything to them, except for three pounds to John Robinson's granddaughter Marcye and an extra 40 shillings for his servant John Irish Jr., if he served out the rest of his contract.

Standish left his heirs in a fairly comfortable position. Willison writes that he "had prospered in the New World" and that his estate was worth what would have been considered a large amount at the time. According to a listing of the items in his estate, it included such things as various livestock, weapons such as muskets, a sword and a cutlass, and just over 40 books in what T. C. Porteus in *Miles Standish: His Lost Lands and Lancashire Connections* calls "a soldier's library. . . . Even the volumes that represent pure literature have a military flavour."

More than this, however, he left behind a legacy. His name along with William Bradford's would become the best known in the *Mayflower* saga. Early historians in particular would be willing to overlook his quick temper in praising him. Abbott, for instance, writes, "It has been a constant pleasure to the author to endeavor to rear a worthy tribute to the heroic captain and the noble man," while Goodwin writes, "His services merit our warmest gratitude, and challenge our admiration. He was the man of men whom the Pilgrims most needed to come to them." Besides the historical accounts, poems would be written about him, monuments raised to him, even pop culture references made to him in the centuries following his death.

8

His Legacy

Much of Miles Standish's enduring legacy is a result of Henry Wadsworth Longfellow's famous poem "The Courtship of Miles Standish," published in 1858. In it, Longfellow tells a story in which Standish courts Priscilla Mullins, another real-life *Mayflower* passenger, after Rose's death. Standish is too afraid to make his feelings known to Mullins himself, so he asks his friend John Alden to speak to her on his behalf—not knowing that Alden is in love with her as well. John doesn't want to let his friend down and so agrees to Standish's request. He goes to Mullins and speaks glowingly of Standish, only to have Mullins ask him, in the poem's most famous line, "Why don't you speak for yourself, John?" thus revealing her love for Alden.

Upon learning of this development, Standish distracts himself with his soldierly duties. Out of loyalty to his friend, Alden does not ask for Mullins's hand in marriage. That is, not until word reaches Plymouth that Standish has been killed in battle. Mullins accepts Alden's proposal, and just as the wedding is ending, Standish shows up—he had not been killed after all. Standish wishes his friend well, saying, "Mine is the same hot blood that leaped in the veins of Hugh Standish. / Sensitive, swift to resent, but as swift in atoning for error. / Never so much as now was Miles Standish the friend of John Alden."

Longfellow was one of the most popular poets of his time and "The Courtship of Miles Standish" was "extraordinarily popular, selling a reported ten thousand copies in London in a single day," according to Nathaniel Philbrick in *Mayflower*.

Longfellow claimed to base his poem in historical fact, but there are many historical inaccuracies in the poem—T. C. Porteus lists several of them in *Miles Standish: His Lost Lands and Lancashire Connections*. Besides those inaccuracies, which can be written off as poetic license, there is no evidence that this story took place at all. In fact, Porteus mentions "In the article on Myles Standish, in the *Encyclopedia Britannica*, 11th edition, it is suggested that there was no time for the episode, inasmuch as Standish's second wife, Barbara, must have been summoned to Plymouth a year before the marriage of John Alden to Priscilla Mullins." (Though Porteus does allow that Standish might have had time for a "passing infatuation" before Barbara arrived.)

None of this has stopped historians, reporters, and others from believing the story to be true. Historian John S. C. Abbott, for instance, writes, "Nearly every event which the poet has woven into his harmonious lines, is accurate even in its most minute details." An article from the September 7, 1895 issue of *The New York Times* even takes Mullins's famous line as fact, saying "the Alden house is inhabited by the ninth John Alden, in direct descent from the John to whom Priscilla said, 'Why don't you speak for yourself, John?'"

> ## FAMOUS DESCENDANTS
>
> Longfellow was a descendant of John Alden and Priscilla Mullins, placing him among the many famous people descended from the original *Mayflower* Pilgrims. U.S. presidents John Adams, John Quincy Adams, Zachary Taylor, Ulysses S. Grant, James Garfield, Franklin D. Roosevelt, George H. W. Bush, and George W. Bush all trace their family lines back to *Mayflower* passengers. Miles Standish has had his share of notable descendants as well, including presidents of Dartmouth College and Harvard University, Vice president Dan Quayle, actor Dick Van Dyke, and Revolutionary War hero Deborah Sampson who fought in several battles disguised as a man.

This willingness to take the poem as history can be explained by the fact that, as Philbrick writes, "the Pilgrims came to be known not as they had truly been but as those of the Victorian era wished them to have been." He goes on to say, "With the outbreak of the Civil War a few years later, the public need for a restorative myth of national origins became even more ardent." The poem thus became part of the Pilgrims' history and was taught to American schoolchildren for generations. Without this poem, Miles Standish would undoubtedly not be as well known as he is today.

THE MONUMENT IN DUXBURY

America's fascination with Miles Standish continued after the Civil War, and toward the end of the nineteenth century the town of Duxbury decided to build a monument to their founding father. A Standish Memorial Committee was formed that included descendants of Standish and others. They chose the top of Captain's Hill on

Standish's old farm as the monument site. They then gathered there on August 17, 1871 to consecrate, or formerly set aside, the land for the monument.

The monument was to be huge, rising 150 feet (45.7-m) off the 180-foot-high (54.8-meter-high) hill, with a 14-foot-high (4.2-meter-high) statue of Standish on top. On August 18, *The New York Times* reported that the monument "will be cylindrical, and rest on four massive arches, about twenty feet in height. This part of the structure will be built of block granite edged. . . . The monument will cost $50,000."

A great crowd gathered on October 7, 1872 as the cornerstone of the monument was laid. John S.C. Abbott writes in *Miles Standish: The Puritan Captain*, "It was indeed a gala day in the ancient town of Duxbury. It is estimated that ten thousand people were present." More than a quarter-century later, on July 1, 1899, the monument was first opened to the public, though it was still not finished until years later. Then on July 31, 1909, the completed monument was finally dedicated to the memory of Miles Standish.

The statue stood guard for just 13 more years before nature dealt it a blow. On August 26, 1922, a lightning bolt struck the statue, lopping off Miles Standish's head and his right arm. Not until 1930 would a replacement statue be put in place so Standish could resume his watch over the Duxbury shore.

THE GRAVE SITE

When they dedicated the land for the monument in Duxbury back in 1871, they knew that Standish had been buried somewhere on the farm, but they didn't know exactly where. In the formal speech at the consecration ceremony, General Horace Binney Sargent spoke of Standish's bones which "were laid somewhere on the hillside— perhaps under our unconscious feet."

Stories involving Miles Standish, whether fiction or truth, have overshadowed his contributions to Plymouth colony and instead made him into an amusing, mysterious character. Although most people associate him with shortness and unrequited love, it was his efforts to protect and ensure the survival of Plymouth that built the early foundation of America.

Several years later a story started circulating in the press that Standish's grave might have been found. Caroline B. Hall, a descendant of Standish's, told of a family tradition that Miles had been buried in the Hall's Corner cemetery in Duxbury and that his grave was marked on either end by two three-cornered stones. Around 1889 a grave matching this description was found, but when they dug it up, they found a woman's bones. Not to be discouraged, some said that these were probably the bones of Miles's daughter Lora or daughter-in-law Mary—he had requested in his will to be buried near them. More digging was done and the bones of a man were found, leading to the stories in the press. At least one reporter was not convinced, however: In the May 26, 1889 issue of the *Boston Daily Globe*, the reporter wrote, "The people of Duxbury are amused at the story of the finding of Myles Standish's grave. . . . Historians generally have agreed that the probably resting place of the old pilgrim is on Harden hill."

In 1891 a group of people returned to the cemetery with permission to open up some more graves. Among that group was Eugene Joseph Vincent Huiginn, who in his book *The Graves of Myles Standish and Other Pilgrims* gives evidence as to why they believed that the graves they found in 1889 were Lora's and Miles's, and how in 1891 they found another woman's grave plus those of two young boys. They believed these new skeletons to be those of Mary plus Miles's sons Charles and John. The book, published in 1914, seems to have not ended the debate at that time, however—on June 18, 1923 an article in *The New York Times* reported that three skeletons dug up in South Duxbury might be that of Miles, Lora, and Mary. "Uncertainty has existed as to where the Plymouth Captain was buried," the article said.

Eventually people came to accept the opinion of Huiginn and his group and the mystery of Standish's grave was considered settled. In 1931 Miles's bones were dug up again, this time to be placed "in a hermetically sealed casket and laid away in a new concrete tomb as a permanent resting place," according to an April 26, 1931 article in the *Washington Post*. The article continued, "The grave of Capt Standish was flag decked today, and on each corner of the plot an old gun was mounted." The grave monument still stands today in the oldest maintained cemetery in the United States, Duxbury's Myles Standish Burying Ground.

CONCLUSION

Miles Standish may not be as well known today as he was in the nine-teenth or even the early twentieth century, but he has remained one of the most famous figures in the story of Plymouth Plantation, earn-ing popular culture references in both the cartoon "A Charlie Brown Thanksgiving" and a song by the rock group R.E.M. The enduring interest in Miles Standish is a result of the man's colorful life and many contradictions. Enough is known about him to make him interesting, but the information is sufficiently limited to allow historians, poets, and others to adapt him to their purposes. His true relationship to the Sepa-ratist Church, for example, still remains a mystery. On the one hand, he remained with the highly religious Pilgrims even after other colonies started up, but as Robert Merrill Bartlett points out in *The Faith of the Pilgrims*, Standish voted for freedom of religion in Plymouth in 1945. Likewise, his son became a deacon at Duxbury, but toward the end of his life when he was choosing executors of his will, "he had chosen none of the Saints, but . . . two of the most liberal men in the colony, both of whom were later disenfranchised for protesting the violent bigotry of some of the Saints," according to Willison in *Saints and Strangers*.

Other contradictions led to his reputations as both an unpredict-able force and a reliable leader, both hot-tempered and cool under pressure. Willison says he was "easily provoked and not to be trusted in matters of high policy," while General Sargent said in his speech at the monument consecration ceremony that, "ultimately his repute in affairs both civil and military was such that he was for many years the Treasurer of the Colony, and during a period of difficulty their agent in England."

Whatever characteristics made up the man, Miles Standish proved to be uniquely suited to ensuring the survival of the colony against incredible odds. Had he not been on the *Mayflower*, it's likely Plymouth would have failed, and the history of an entire continent, and therefore the world, would look very different.

Chronology

ca 1584	Born in Lancashire, England, or perhaps Isle of Man.
1609	Pilgrims settle in Leiden, Holland.
1620	The *Mayflower* embarks from Plymouth, England and anchors in Provincetown Harbor, Cape Cod; First encounter with Native

TIMELINE

1620 The *Mayflower* embarks from England

1626 With seven others, assumes the debt of the Plymouth colony

1632 Cofounds settlement of Duxbury

1584

1633

c. 1584 Born in Lancashire, England, or perhaps Isle of Man

1621 Chosen as official military commander of New Plymouth colony; "First Thanksgiving" harvest celebration with Wampanoag

1633 Chosen as assistant governor of Plymouth

Americans; Pilgrims choose an abandoned Wampanoag village for their settlement.

1621   Rose Standish dies; Chosen as official military commander of New Plymouth colony; Pilgrims meet Samoset and Tisquantum (Squanto); Governor John Carver and the Wampanoag leader Massasoit sign peace treaty; "First Thanksgiving" harvest celebration with Wampanoag.

1622   Narragansett tribe threatens the colony; Wall built around town.

1623   Slaying of Pecksuot and Wituwamat at Wessagusset; The future Barbara Standish arrives on the *Anne*, marries Miles later that year.

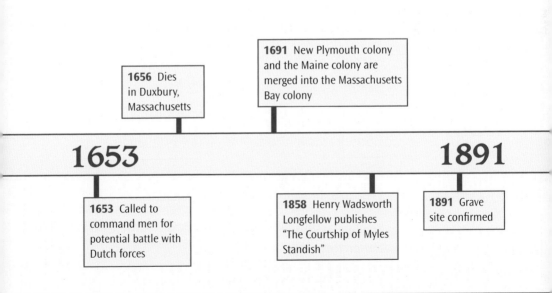

1656 Dies in Duxbury, Massachusetts

1691 New Plymouth colony and the Maine colony are merged into the Massachusetts Bay colony

1653

1891

1653 Called to command men for potential battle with Dutch forces

1858 Henry Wadsworth Longfellow publishes "The Courtship of Myles Standish"

1891 Grave site confirmed

1624	Probable birth year of son Charles.
1625	Encounter at Cape Ann; Returns to England to meet with Council of New England.
1626	Returns to New Plymouth; With seven others, assumes the debt of the Plymouth colony.
1627	Probable birth year of sons John and Alexander.
1628	Arrests Thomas Morton of Merrymount; Probable birth year of daughter Lora.
1629	Probable birth year of son Myles.
1632	Cofounds settlement of Duxbury.
1633	Chosen as assistant governor of Plymouth; Probable birth year of son Josias.
1634	Chosen again as assistant governor of Plymouth; Possible birth year of second Charles.
1635	Chosen again as assistant governor of Plymouth; Encounter with French traders at Penobscot.
1637	Duxbury incorporated as a separate town.
1642	Beginning of the first English Civil War, which ends the Great Migration to the New World.
1644	Chosen as colony treasurer; Elder William Brewster dies.
1645	Prepares for war with the Narragansetts.
1653	Called to command men for potential battle with Dutch forces.
1655	Edward Winslow dies of fever while at sea.
1656	Dies in Duxbury, Massachusetts.

1691	The New Plymouth colony and the Maine colony are merged into the Massachusetts Bay colony.
1858	Henry Wadsworth Longfellow publishes "The Courtship of Myles Standish."
1871	Construction begins on Standish monument in Duxbury.
1891	Grave site confirmed.

Bibliography

BOOKS

Abbott, John S. C. *Miles Standish, The Puritan Captain*. New York: Dodd, Mead and Company, 1898.

Bartlett, Robert Merrill. *The Faith of the Pilgrims*. New York: United Church Press, 1978.

Bradford, William. *Governor William Bradford's Letter Book*. Boston: Massachusetts Society of Mayflower Descendants, 1906.

Bradford, William. *Of Plymouth Plantation*. New York: Alfred A. Knopf, 1970.

Caffrey, Kate. *The Mayflower*. Briarcliff Manor, N.Y.: Stein and Day, 1974.

Crawford, Mary Caroline. *In the Days of the Pilgrim Fathers*. Boston: Little, Brown, and Company, 1920.

Davis, William T. *History of the Town of Plymouth*. Philadelphia: J. W. Lewis & Co., 1885.

Dillon, Francis. *The Pilgrims*. Golden City, N.Y.: Doubleday & Company, Inc., 1973.

Fleming, Thomas J. *One Small Candle: The Pilgrim's First Year in America*. New York: W. W. Norton & Company, Inc., 1963.

Goodwin, John A. *The Pilgrim Republic*. Boston: Ticknor and Company, 1888.

Harrison, William. *Harrison's Description of England in Shakespere's Youth*. London, England: N. Trübner & Co., 1877.

Hubbard, William. *A General History of New England*. Boston: Charles C. Little and James Brown, 1848.

Huiginn, Eugene Joseph Vincent. *The Graves of Myles Standish and Other Pilgrims*. Beverly, Mass.: Published by the author, 1914.

Kossman, E.H. and A.F. Mellink, editors. *Texts Concerning the Revolt of the Netherlands*. Cambridge, England: Cambridge University Press, 1974.

Longfellow, Henry Wadsworth. *The Poems of Longfellow*. New York: The Modern Library, 1967.

Morton, Nathaniel. *New England's Memorial*. Boston: Congregational Board of Publication, 1855.

Philbrick, Nathaniel. *Mayflower: A Story of Courage, Community, and War*. New York: Viking, 2006.

Porteus, Thomas Cruddas, B.A., B.D. *Captain Myles Standish: His Lost Lands and Lancashire Connections*. Manchester, England: University Press, 1920.

Prince, Thomas. *A Chronological History of New-England*. Boston: Antiquarian Bookstore, 1852.

Raleigh, Sir Walter. *The Works of Sir Walter Raleigh, Kt, Vol. V*. Oxford, England: University Press, 1829.

Scott, Henry Edwards, editor. *The New England Historical and Genealogical Register, Vol. 68*. Boston: The New England Historic Genealogical Society, 1914.

Wagenknecht, Edward. *Henry Wadsworth Longfellow: Portrait of an American Humanist*. Oxford, England: University Press, 1966.

Willison, George F. *The Pilgrim Reader*. Golden City, N.Y.: Doubleday & Company, Inc., 1953.

Willison, George F. *Saints and Strangers*. New York: Reynal & Hitchcock, 1945.

Winsor, Justin. *History of the Town of Duxbury, Massachusetts*. Boston: Crosby & Nichols, 1849.

Young, G. V. C. *Pilgrim Myles Standish, First Manx American*. Isle of Man: Manx-Svenska Publishing Company, 1984.

WEB SITES

"Elizabethan Timeline," Elizabethan-Era.org. Available online. URL: http://www.elizabethan-era.org.uk/elizabethan-timeline.htm. Updated March 20, 2008.

"The Evolution of Thanksgiving," Pilgrim Hall Museum. Available online. URL: http://www.pilgrimhall.org/thnkevol.htm.

"Famous Descendants of Mayflower Passengers," MayflowerHistory.com. Available online. URL: http://www.mayflowerhistory.com/Genealogy/famousdescendants.php.

"The First Thanksgiving at Plymouth," Pilgrim Hall Museum. Available online. URL: http://www.pilgrimhall.org/f_thanks.htm.

"Mayflower Passenger Deaths, 1620–1621," The Plymouth Colony Archive Project. Available online. URL: http://www.histarch.uiuc.edu/plymouth/Maydeaths.html.

"Myles Standish Site in Leiden Threatened," RootsWeb. Available online. URL: http://listsearches.rootsweb.com/th/read/STANDISH/2000-12/0977189911. Posted December 18, 2000.

"Myles Standish, Born Where? The State of the Question," by Dr. Jeremy Dupertuis Bangs, Sail1620.org. Available online. URL: http://www.sail1620.org/history/35-biographies/51-myles-standish.html.

"Pilgrim Father Captain Myles Standish of Duxbury Lancashire and Massachusetts," by Helen Moorwood, Duxbury.Plus.com. Available online. URL: http://www.duxbury.plus.com/bard/mstand/index.htm.

"Pilgrim History," MayflowerHistory.com. Available online. URL: http://www.mayflowerhistory.com/History/history.php.

"Presidential Thanksgiving Proclamations 1789–1815: George Washington, John Adams, James Madison," Pilgrim Hall Museum. Available online. URL: http://www.pilgrimhall.org/ThanxProc1789.htm.

"Probate Inventory for Estate of Myles Standish, 1656/1657," The Plymouth Colony Archive Project. Available online. URL: http://www.histarch.uiuc.edu/plymouth/Pstandish.html.

"Welcome to Duxbury Massachusetts," Town of Duxbury, Massachusetts. Available online. URL: http://www.town.duxbury.ma.us/Public_Documents/DuxburyMA_WebDocs/about.

"Will of Myles Standish," MayflowerHistory.com. Available online. URL: http://www.mayflowerhistory.com/PrimarySources/WillsAndProbates/MylesStandish.php.

NEWSPAPERS

"Bolt Beheads Myles Standish Statue on Duxbury Shore." *Boston Daily Globe*, August 27, p. 18.

"The Great Captain's Grave." *Boston Daily Globe*, May 26, 1889, p. 4.

"Myles Standish: Great Memorial Celebration at Duxbury, Mass." *The New York Times*, August 18, 1871, p. 5.

"Myles Standish Resumes Vigil over Plymouth." *Christian Science Monitor*, November 26, 1930, p. 2.

"Myles Standish's Grave." *Boston Daily Globe*, November 5, 1891, p. 10.

"No Man Knoweth." *Boston Daily Globe*, May 30, 1891, p. 5.

"The Puritan Captain." *Boston Daily Globe*, October 8, 1872, p. 8.

"Standish Monument at Duxbury." *Boston Daily Globe*, July 18, 1909, p. SM5.

"Standish Monument Opened." *Boston Daily Globe*, July 2, 1899, p. 18.

"Standish's Grave Again Disturbed." *The Washington Post*, April 26, 1931, p. M17.

"Suspect Skeleton Dug Up Is That of Myles Standish." *The New York Times*, June 18, 1923.

"Where Capt Miles Standish Lies." *Boston Daily Globe*, June 18, 1896, p. 8.

Special Thanks to Stephen O'Neill, Associate Director/Curator of Pilgrim Hall Museum, Plymouth, Mass.

Further Resources

Johnson, Caleb. "Pilgrim History," MayflowerHistory.com. Available online. URL: http://www.mayflowerhistory.com/History/history.php.

Longfellow, Henry Wadsworth. *The Poems of Longfellow*. New York: The Modern Library, 1967.

Philbrick, Nathaniel. *The Mayflower & the Pilgrims' New World*. New York: G. P. Putnam's Sons, 2008.

"The Pilgrim Story," Pilgrim Hall Museum. Available online. URL: http://www.pilgrimhall.org/museum.htm.

Stratton, Eugene Aubrey. *Plymouth Colony, Its History & People, 1620–1691*. Salt Lake City, Utah: Ancestry Publishing, 1986.

Wilbur, C. Keith. *The New England Indians*, 2nd Edition. Guilford, Conn.: Globe Pequot Press, 1996.

Picture Credits

Index

About the Author

Daniel K. Davis lives in San Francisco with his wife, Carrie, and their son Cai. He graduated from the University of California, Berkeley with a bachelor's degree in English, which he is doing his best to put to good use. This is his second book.